CUB0926736

PIERS GAVESTON

PIERS GAVESTON

EDWARD II'S ADOPTIVE BROTHER

PIERRE CHAPLAIS

CLARENDON PRESS · OXFORD
1994

Oxford University Press, Walton Street, Oxford OX2 6DP

Oxford New York Toronto
Delhi Bombay Calcutta Madras Karachi
Kuala Lumpur Singapore Hong Kong Tokyo
Nairobi Dar es Salaam Cape Town
Melbourne Auckland Madrid
and associated companies in
Berlin Ibadan

Oxford is a trade mark of Oxford University Press

Published in the United States
by Oxford University Press Inc., New York

British Library Cataloguing in Publication Data
Data available

Library of Congress Cataloging in Publication Data
Chaplais, Pierre.
Piers Gaveston: Edward II's adoptive brother / Pierre Chaplais.
p. cm.
Includes bibliographical references and index.
1. Gaveston, Piers, ca. 1284–1312. 2. Great Britain—Court and
courtiers—Biography. 3. Great Britain—History—Edward II,
1307–1327. 4. Favorites, Royal—Great Britain—Biography.
5. Edward II, King of England, 1284–1327. I. Title.
DA231.G2C48 1994
942.03'6'092—dc20 93–37540
ISBN 0–19–820449–3

1 3 5 7 9 10 8 6 4 2

Typeset by Cambrian Typesetters Frimley, Surrey
Printed in Great Britain
on acid-free paper by
Bookcraft Ltd.
Midsomer Norton, Avon

PREFACE

THIS book developed from a paper read at a meeting of the Medieval Group in All Souls College, Oxford, on 23 November 1990, under the chairmanship of Professor G. A. Holmes, Chichele Professor of Medieval History. I am very grateful to Professor Holmes for giving me the opportunity to air my views on Gaveston's relationship with Edward II, and to those who attended the meeting for their comments.

The plates are reproduced by kind permission of the Controller of Her Majesty's Stationery Office (Plate I), the British Library (Plate II), the Dean and Chapter of Canterbury (Plate III), and the Provost and Fellows of Oriel College, Oxford (Plate IV). For their help with the consultation and photography of the material reproduced, and for other assistance, I am very grateful to Dr Elizabeth Hallam and Dr David Crook of the Public Record Office, Mrs Charlotte Hodgson and Miss Anne Oakley of the Canterbury Cathedral Archives, and Dr Jeremy Catto and Mrs Elizabeth Boardman of Oriel College, Oxford.

Crown Copyright material (notably Appendix II) is printed by permission of the Controller of Her Majesty's Stationery Office. Excerpts from a particularly important document in the Westminster Abbey Muniments (Appendix I) are printed by courtesy of the Dean and Chapter of Westminster. For allowing me to consult this document in the original and in a photographic reproduction, I am grateful to Dr Richard Mortimer, Keeper of the Muniments, and Mrs Enid Nixon.

To the two anonymous readers who were consulted by the Oxford University Press before publication I owe much sound advice, which helped to improve this book. My greatest debt is to Miss Barbara Harvey, who read the whole of the book in draft and also the proofs, and made invaluable suggestions not only on matters connected with Westminster Abbey, but also on the general structure of the book, and to Dr C. S. L. Davies, who also read the book in draft and contributed much constructive criticism.

I also wish to thank Dr John Maddicott for his support and helpful comments. My indebtedness to his book on Thomas of Lancaster will be evident from the many references to it in the footnotes. Others kindly assisted on individual points: Mr James Campbell, Dr David Howlett and his staff at the Oxford office of the *Dictionary of Medieval Latin,* and Dr M. K. Lawson. Among the friends who listened patiently over many months to what I had to say on the deeds and misdeeds of Piers Gaveston, and offered valuable comments, I wish to mention in particular Miss Susan Burdell and Miss Valerie Lawrence of the History Faculty Library, who also assisted with bibliographical problems. Finally, I should like to express my gratitude to Miss Sophie MacCallum and Miss Helen Gray of the Oxford University Press, who helped with the final preparation of the book.

P. C.
Wadham College, Oxford
April 1993

CONTENTS

LIST OF PLATES

(between pp. 18 and 19)

ABBREVIATIONS

Ann. Lond.	*Annales Londonienses*, in *Chronicles of the Reigns of Edward I and Edward II*, i, ed. W. Stubbs (RS, 1882)
Ann. Paul.	*Annales Paulini*, in *Chronicles of the Reigns of Edward I and Edward II*, i, ed. W. Stubbs (RS, 1882)
BIHR	*Bulletin of the Institute of Historical Research*
Birch	W. de Gray Birch, *Catalogue of Seals in the Department of Manuscripts in the British Museum*, i (1887)
BL	British Library, London
Bodl. Lib.	Bodleian Library, Oxford
Bridlington	*Gesta Edwardi de Carnarvan, auctore canonico Bridlingtoniensi*, in *Chronicles of the Reigns of Edward I and Edward II*, ii, ed. W. Stubbs (RS, 1883)
Brit. Chron.	*Handbook of British Chronology*, ed. E. B. Fryde, D. E. Greenway, S. Porter, and I. Roy, 3rd edn. (Royal Historical Society, Guides and Handbooks, ii, 1986)
Cal. Chanc. War. i	*Calendar of Chancery Warrants preserved in the Public Record Office*, i (AD 1244–1326)
CChR	*Calendar of the Charter Rolls preserved in the Public Record Office*
CCR	*Calendar of the Close Rolls preserved in the Public Record Office*
CFR	*Calendar of the Fine Rolls preserved in the Public Record Office*
Chaplais, *EMDA*	Pierre Chaplais, *Essays in Medieval Diplomacy and Administration* (London, 1981)
Chaplais, *EMDP* i	—— *English Medieval Diplomatic Practice*, part i: *Documents and Interpretation*, 2 vols. (HMSO, 1982)
Chaplais, *ERD*	—— *English Royal Documents, King John–Henry VI* (Oxford, 1971)
CLR	*Calendar of the Liberate Rolls preserved in the Public Record Office*
Cole, *Documents*	*Documents Illustrative of English History in the Thirteenth and Fourteenth Centuries*, ed. Henry Cole (London, 1844)

Conway Davies, Baron. Opp.	James Conway Davies, *The Baronial Opposition to Edward II* (Cambridge University Press, 1918)
CPL ii	*Calendar of Entries in the Papal Registers relating to Great Britain and Ireland, Papal Letters*, ii (AD 1305–42), ed. W. H. Bliss (HMSO, 1895)
CPR	*Calendar of the Patent Rolls preserved in the Public Record Office*
EHR	*English Historical Review*
Florence of Worcester, i	*Florentii Wigorniensis monachi Chronicon ex Chronicis*, ed. B. Thorpe, i (English Historical Society, London, 1848)
Flores, iii	*Flores Historiarum*, ed. H. R. Luard, iii (RS, 1890)
Foedera: R	*Foedera, conventiones, literae . . .*, ed. Thomas Rymer, 4 vols. in 7 parts (Rec. Comm., 1816–69)
Gaveston's Jewels	*Edward II, the Lords Ordainers, and Piers Gaveston's Jewels and Horses*, ed. R. A. Roberts (Camden Miscellany xv, Royal Historical Society, Camden 3rd Series, xli, 1929)
Guisborough	*The Chronicle of Walter of Guisborough*, ed. Harry Rothwell (Royal Historical Society, Camden 3rd Series, lxxxix, 1957)
Hallam, *Itinerary*	Elizabeth M. Hallam, *The Itinerary of Edward II and his Household* (List and Index Society, ccxi, 1984)
Hamilton, *Gaveston*	J. S. Hamilton, *Piers Gaveston, Earl of Cornwall, 1307–1312* (Wayne State University Press, 1988)
Harvey, *Wenlok*	*Documents Illustrating the Rule of Walter de Wenlok, Abbot of Westminster, 1283–1307*, ed. Barbara F. Harvey (Royal Historical Society, Camden 4th Series, ii, 1965)
Henry of Huntingdon	*Henrici Archidiaconi Huntendunensis Historia Anglorum*, ed. T. Arnold (RS, 1879)
Higden, *Polychronicon*, viii	*Polychronicon Ranulphi Higden, monachi Cestrensis*, viii, ed. J. R. Lumby (RS, 1882)
Isabella's Household Book	*The Household Book of Queen Isabella of England*, ed. F. D. Blackley and G. Hermansen (University of Alberta Press, 1971)
Johnstone, *Edw. of Carnarvon*	Hilda Johnstone, *Edward of Carnarvon, 1284–1307* (Manchester University Press, 1946)
Keen, 'Brotherhood in Arms'	Maurice Keen, 'Brotherhood in Arms', *History*, 47 (1962), 1–17
Lanercost	*Chronicon de Lanercost*, ed. Joseph Stevenson (Edinburgh, 1839)

Liber Quot.	*Liber Quotidianus Contrarotulatoris Garderobae anno regni regis Edwardi Primi vicesimo octavo* (Society of Antiquaries, London, 1787)
Maddicott, *Lancaster*	J. R. Maddicott, *Thomas of Lancaster* (Oxford University Press, 1970)
Maxwell-Lyte, *Great Seal*	H. C. Maxwell-Lyte, *Historical Notes on the Use of the Great Seal of England* (HMSO, 1926)
Melsa, ii	*Chronica Monasterii de Melsa*, ed. E. A. Bond, ii (RS, 1867)
Murimuth	*Adae Murimuth Continuatio Chronicarum*, ed. E. M. Thompson (RS, 1889)
NS	New Series
Palgrave, *Antient Kalendars*	*The Antient Kalendars and Inventories of the Treasury of His Majesty's Exchequer . . .*, ed. F. Palgrave, 3 vols. (Rec. Comm., 1836)
Parl. Writs.	*The Parliamentary Writs and Writs of Military Summons . . .*, ed. F. Palgrave, 2 vols. in 4 (Rec. Comm., 1827–34)
Pearce, *The Monks of Westminster*	E. H. Pearce, *The Monks of Westminster* (Cambridge University Press, 1916)
Phillips, *Pembroke*	J. R. S. Phillips, *Aymer de Valence, Earl of Pembroke* (Oxford, 1972)
PRO	Public Record Office, London
Rec. Comm.	Record Commission
Reg. Henrici Woodlock	*Registrum Henrici Woodlock, diocesis Wintoniensis, A.D. 1305–1316*, ed. A. W. Goodman, 2 vols. (Canterbury and York Society, 1940–1)
Reg. Ricardi de Swinfield	*Registrum Ricardi de Swinfield, episcopi Herefordensis, A.D. 1283–1317*, ed. W. W. Capes (Canterbury and York Society, 1909)
Reg. Simonis de Gandavo	*Registrum Simonis de Gandavo, diocesis Saresbiriensis, A.D. 1297–1315*, ed. C. T. Flower and M. C. B. Dawes, i (Canterbury and York Society, 1934)
Richardson and Sayles, *The Governance of Mediaeval England*	H. G. Richardson and G. O. Sayles, *The Governance of Mediaeval England from the Conquest to Magna Carta* (Edinburgh University Press, 1963)
Rot. Parl.	*Rotuli Parliamentorum*
RS	Rolls Series
Statutes, i	*Statutes of the Realm*, i (1810)
Tout, *Chapters*	T. F. Tout, *Chapters in the Administrative History of*

	Mediaeval England, 6 vols. (Manchester University Press, 1920–33)
Tout, *Place of Edw. II*	—— *The Place of the Reign of Edward II in English History*, 2nd edn. (Manchester University Press, 1936)
Trivet	*Nicolai Triveti Annalium Continuatio*, ed. A. Hall (Oxford, 1722)
Trokelowe	*Johannis de Trokelowe et Henrici de Blaneford . . . Chronica et Annales*, ed. H. T. Riley (RS, 1866)
Two of the Saxon Chronicles Parallel, ed. Plummer	*Two of the Saxon Chronicles Parallel*, ed. C. Plummer, 2 vols. (Oxford, 1952)
Vita	*Vita Edwardi Secundi*, ed. N. Denholm-Young (Nelson's Medieval Texts, 1957)
Walsingham, *Hist. Anglicana*, i	*Thomae Walsingham, quondam monachi S. Albani, Historia Anglicana*, ed. H. T. Riley, i (RS, 1863)
WAM	Westminster Abbey Muniments
William of Malmesbury, *Gesta Regum*, i	*Willelmi Malmesbiriensis monachi de Gestis Regum Anglorum libri quinque*, ed. W. Stubbs, i (RS, 1887)
Wyon	A. B. Wyon and A. Wyon, *The Great Seals of England* (London, 1887)
Zutshi, *Original Papal Letters in England, 1305–1415*	*Original Papal Letters in England, 1305–1415*, ed. P. N. R. Zutshi, Index Actorum Romanorum Pontificum, v (Vatican, 1990)

INTRODUCTION

A RELUCTANT KING AND HIS *ALTER EGO*

THE most contemptuous remark that could be made about any king and was actually made about Edward II by his contemporaries was that he was an incompetent ruler. In 1327 this criticism was regarded as so decisive an argument for the king's removal from office that it was placed at the head of the complaints lodged against him by the Hilary parliament in the 'Articles of Deposition'. The first of these articles claimed that the king was not competent to govern ('nest pas suffisaunt de governer'), for in all his time he had been led and ruled by others, who had advised him badly to his own dishonour, and to the destruction of the Church and of all his people; he had neither made any effort to see or find out what was good or bad, nor taken any steps to remedy the situation when requested to do so by the great and wise men of the kingdom. The second article continued in the same vein: during all his reign, the king had been unwilling to take or believe good advice, and, instead of devoting his efforts to good government, he had spent all his time in unseemly pursuits, neglecting the dispatch of the affairs of the kingdom.[1]

Although the Articles of Deposition may have been intended mainly for propaganda purposes and their text is known only from the slightly later *Apologia* of Bishop Adam de Orleton, dating from 1334, there is no reason to doubt their authenticity. Regarding the accusation of incompetence against the king, the Bridlington chronicle confirms that the Westminster parliament of Hilary 1327 declared

---

[1] *Foedera*: R. II. i. 650; R. Twysden, *Historiae Anglicanae Scriptores Decem* (London, 1652), col. 2765.

that the king, having on numerous occasions acted unadvisedly, was deemed unfit ('minus sufficientem') for the royal office.[2] In any case, in 1327 the accusation was not new. As early as January 1313, a former sheriff of Cornwall, John de Bedewynd, was brought before the king's council, sitting in the exchequer, charged with stating publicly in full county court at Lostwithiel that the king had evil councillors and that he had been badly advised when he granted to Antonio di Pessagno the purchase of tin in the county of Cornwall; Bedewynd had apparently pronounced (either in words or by implication) that the king himself and his council were incompetent ('inueniendo insufficienciam in ipso domino Rege et consilio suo').[3]

It seems quite remarkable that the king's competence should have been disputed on the ground that he asked for the advice of others instead of making his own decisions. The fact that he relied on 'evil' rather than good councillors, and that their advice turned out, not unexpectedly, to be bad was in a sense irrelevant to the assessment of the king's competence; it simply made the disaster of his inadequacy greater. In the words of the canon of Bridlington and of Higden, as well as of the later chronicler of Meaux, who copied them, the king followed the advice of others rather than his own judgement, a remark which, in the context in which it occurs, was without doubt meant to be disparaging, not complimentary.[4]

None of this appears to make sense unless we assume that the matters at issue belonged to the king's prerogative and as such were his own responsibility, that of no one else, and required his own personal intervention. Edward was quite happy, as he was expected to be, to leave the routine government to his chancellor, treasurer, and other ministers. But it irked him that there were still some decisions which he had to take himself; those, too, he wanted to pass on to someone else. He had a passion for breeding horses, digging and ditching, rowing and swimming, and generally for rural occupations and mechanical arts, all of which were regarded as unfit for a king,

---

[2] *Bridlington*, p. 90.

[3] Conway Davies, *Baron. Opp.*, pp. 28, 329, 553 (no. 19); Phillips, *Pembroke*, p. 53. The charges against Bedewynd, which had been brought by Pessagno himself, were not necessarily true, as Pessagno was not averse to slander (Conway Davies, *Baron. Opp.*, p. 112 and n. 7; Phillips, *Pembroke*, pp. 181–2).

[4] *Bridlington*, p. 91: 'magis alieno quam proprio consilio credens'; Higden, *Polychronicon*, viii. 298: 'magis alienum quam proprium consilium sequens'; *Melsa*, ii. 280: 'magis alienum quam proprium consilium sequens'.

but he did not care for governing the kingdom.[5] His interests were reflected in the company he kept: he had no wish to spend his time with magnates (*proceres*); he preferred to consort with singers, actors, oarsmen, diggers, etc., who shared his tastes.[6]

It looks as if Edward was not so much an incompetent king as a reluctant one; he wanted a deputy to whom he could delegate the exercise of the royal prerogative. His choice, of course, had to fall on someone he fully trusted, preferably, to parody a biblical expression, someone he loved like himself, as Jonathan loved David. During the first five years of his reign, Edward's deputy was Piers Gaveston. The *Annales Paulini*, to which we owe this unexpected identification, add that it made everybody very angry that there should thus be two kings reigning jointly in one kingdom, one in name and the other in deed.[7] The identification is confirmed by other sources, which, although less specific than the *Annales Paulini*, state either that Gaveston made himself the king's equal, accroaching royal power and giving bad advice to the king, or that he did not regard anyone else in England as his equal except the king, or that he behaved almost like a second king, who was above everyone and had no equal.[8] At the end of the reign, Hugh le Despenser the younger played the same role as Gaveston had done, and was accused of the same crimes, namely accroaching royal power and dignity, and counselling the king badly; he was like the king's 'right eye' and he conducted himself like a second king.[9] Gaveston was the first of Edward's two so-called favourites, and Despenser the second. Both are alleged to have had a homosexual relationship with the king[10] and both were executed for treason.

Although a detailed comparative study of the two men might produce interesting results, the present book is concerned exclusively with Gaveston. It does not pretend to supersede the full biography

[5] Conway Davies, *Baron. Opp.*, p. 77; Hilda Johnstone, 'The Eccentricities of Edward II', *EHR* 48 (1933), 264–7; ead., *Edw. of Carnarvon*, pp. 17, 129–30.

[6] *Bridlington*, p. 91; Higden, *Polychronicon*, viii. 298; *Melsa*, ii. 280.

[7] *Ann. Paul.*, p. 259; below, ch. 5 n. 62.

[8] *Bridlington*, p. 34; Richardson and Sayles, *The Governance of Mediaeval England*, p. 468; *Vita*, pp. 1, 14; *Ann. Lond.*, p. 152.

[9] Conway Davies, *Baron. Opp.*, p. 104 nn. 5–6; *BIHR* 58 (1985), 98 (compare line 5: 'a les graces a droit' and below, ch. 5 n. 62: 'diversa genera gratiarum').

[10] Regarding Despenser, see *Chroniques de Jean Froissart*, ed. Siméon Luce, i (Société de l'histoire de France, 1869), 34.

recenty published by J. S. Hamilton, *Piers Gaveston, Earl of Cornwall, 1307–1312* (Detroit, 1988), but concentrates on such aspects of Gaveston's life and career as seemed to warrant further investigations and invite new thinking.

On Gaveston's origins and early years little can be added to the comments of Hamilton and those of Hilda Johnstone in her *Edward of Carnarvon, 1284–1307* (Manchester University Press, 1946). Piers was a younger son of Arnaud, lord of Gabaston in Béarn, on the southern fringe of English Gascony, and of Clarmonde de Marsan. Since Edward of Carnarvon (born on 25 April 1284) and he are said to have been contemporaries (*coetanei*),[11] Piers was probably born in the early 1280s. His childhood cannot have been a happy one. He hardly had the chance to know his mother, who died before February 1288 and possibly even before February 1287, when he was only a few years old.[12] His father Arnaud, a knight (*cavoirs*) by 1272,[13] was too busy in Edward I's service in the 1280s and 1290s to have spent much time with Piers: he fought in Edward's Welsh campaign of 1282–3 and was used twice by him as a hostage, the first time in Aragon in 1288–9 and the second time in France from February 1294 to November 1296, when he escaped to England.[14] How Piers spent those years is unknown, but his arrival in England seems to have coincided with his father's escape. At any rate, he took part in Edward I's expedition to Flanders in 1297, when he probably was in his early teens. He was then a yeoman (*valettus* or *scutifer*) in the king's household. Wherever Edward of Carnarvon and he met for the first time, it was not in Flanders, because Edward remained in England as regent while his father was on the Continent.[15]

In 1300 Piers was transferred to the household of the younger Edward; they fought side by side in the Scottish campaign of that year. It may have been then, as suggested by Hilda Johnstone, that the two young men became intimate friends.[16] They had a great deal

---

[11] Trokelowe, p. 64.

[12] *Rôles gascons*, ii, ed. C. Bémont, nos. 641, 975; iii, ed. Bémont, p. clxxxiii.

[13] *Recueil d'actes relatifs à l'administration des rois d'Angleterre en Guyenne au XIIIe siècle*, ed. C. Bémont (Paris, 1914), no. 470.

[14] Hamilton, *Gaveston*, pp. 22–4; J.-P. Trabut-Cussac, *L'Administration anglaise en Gascogne sous Henry III et Edouard I de 1254 à 1307* (Paris, 1972), pp. 91–2.

[15] Johnstone, *Edw. of Carnarvon*, pp. 35–42; Hamilton, *Gaveston*, p. 29.

[16] Johnstone, *Edw. of Carnarvon*, p. 54.

in common. Like Piers, Edward had not had a particularly happy childhood. Like him, he had been starved of affection in his tender years. He, too, had hardly known his mother, Eleanor of Castile: she died in 1290, when he was 6 years old, and out of those six years they had been apart for three (1286–9), which she had spent in Gascony with her husband, leaving the young Edward behind in England.

What kind of human relationship was there between Gaveston and Edward of Carnarvon before and after the latter's accession to the throne? Was it one of the rare great friendships in history, similar to that which existed between David and Jonathan, Achilles and Patroclus, Roland and Oliver, and other well-known heroes? Or was it of a homosexual nature, or a mixture of the two? Or was it something completely different? As has been rightly said, no conclusive proof will ever be found which will enable us to answer these questions positively, but we can at least give tentative answers, and this is what has been attempted in this book.

All the main events in Gaveston's life from 1307 to 1312 have been examined by reviewing the evidence available in chronicles as well as in official records. It is particularly unfortunate that none of the chronicles of the period is trustworthy in its entirety. Even the generally excellent *Vita Edwardi Secundi* is not faultless: it makes, for example, both Edward and Gaveston spend Christmas in York in 1311, although we know for certain that Edward was then at Westminster. The records themselves need interpretation, among them the famous charter of 6 August 1307, by which Edward II granted the earldom of Cornwall to Gaveston. What is the meaning, for example, of the extraordinary decoration of this charter? To mention only one other point, is it really possible, as has been claimed, that, in official records of the same date, Gaveston was sometimes styled earl of Cornwall, and sometimes not? It is on this critical or 'diplomatic' examination of the relevant records that the emphasis has been placed throughout this book, in the hope that some new light might be thrown on some of the important events concerning both Edward and Gaveston, from the latter's return from exile in August 1307 to the settlement, after his death, of the jewel question in 1313.

I

COMPACT OF BROTHERHOOD

The chronicle evidence

'THERE was not anyone who had a good word to say about the king or Piers,' wrote the chronicler of Lanercost after his account of Edward II's coronation in 1308[1] This may have been a slight exaggeration, but all the chroniclers of the reign agree in blaming both Edward and Gaveston for all the ills which afflicted the kingdom from 1307 to 1312. The blame, of course, was not equally apportioned between them: most of it was laid at the door of Gaveston, whose extravagance and greed bankrupted the king's treasury,[2] who made enemies of the earls by his insults and arrogance,[3] and above all gave evil counsel to the king;[4] all these charges were made more heinous and at the same time more credible by labelling the accused, somewhat unfairly, a foreigner.[5] The king's main fault was that he listened only too readily to Gaveston's counsel instead of taking the advice of his English barons;[6] as a result, after six years on the throne, Edward had accomplished nothing worthwhile, apart from marrying into another royal house and producing a fine heir to the throne.[7]

Why was Edward so consistent in his blind support of Gaveston in

---

[1] *Lanercost*, p. 211: 'nec fuit qui de rege vel de Petro aliquid boni loqueretur'.
[2] *Rot. Parl.* i. 283; *Statutes*, i. 162; *Vita*, pp. 6, 40; *Flores*, iii. 142; *Speculum*, 14 (1939), 75–6; Trokelowe, pp. 64, 68; Walsingham, *Hist. Anglicana*, i. 120, 122–3.
[3] *Vita*, pp. 8, 15; *Flores*, iii. 140; Tout, *Place of Edw. II*, p. 12 n.2.
[4] *Rot. Parl.* i. 283; *Vita*, p. 40.
[5] Ibid., pp. 1, 3, 15; Walsingham, *Hist. Anglicana*, i. 120.
[6] *Vita*, pp. 39–40.
[7] Ibid., p. 39.

the face of so much opposition? To this question the answer of the chronicles is unanimous: the king's misguided total trust in Gaveston was due to the unique personal relationship which had existed between them ever since the Gascon joined the household of Edward when or shortly before the latter became prince of Wales. On the exact nature of that relationship the chroniclers are disappointingly vague, purposely so perhaps out of reticence, but much more probably because they genuinely had no clear idea of what really went on between the two men. Most of them simply say that Edward loved Gaveston 'beyond measure', 'beyond measure and reason', or 'uniquely', or that his love or affection for him was 'excessive', 'immoderate', or 'inordinate', and the intimacy between them 'undue' or 'excessive'; 'in love', says the author of the *Vita*, Edward was 'incapable of moderation'.[8]

What makes these references to Edward's excessive love for Gaveston particularly interesting is that they occur, in almost identical terms, in a whole group of contemporary or near-contemporary chronicles, whose authors include the prejudiced Robert of Reading as well as the writer of the *Vita*, who, in this connection as in others, was as fair-minded as anyone could be in the circumstances. This does not mean, however, that the phrase 'excessive love' and its numerous alternatives were interpreted in the same way by all those who used them. It is generally believed that they were meant to hint at the existence of a homosexual relationship between the two men. In so far as Robert of Reading is concerned, a plausible case could perhaps be made for this interpretation, since Robert alludes to the king's love for 'illicit and sinful unions' and to his rejection of the sweet embraces of his wife.[9] In support of the same interpretation one might also quote the *Annales Paulini*, which claim that there was a rumour going around the whole country that 'the king loved an evil male sorcerer more than he did his wife, a most

---

[8] *Ann. Paul.*, p. 255: 'adamaret ... ultra modum'; p. 259: 'pre amore nimio'; Trokelowe, p. 64: 'dilexerat ultra modum'; *Flores*, iii. 331: 'ultra modum et rationem amavit'; *Ann. Lond.*, p. 151: 'unice dilexit'; *Flores*, iii. 146: 'ob immoderati magnitudinem amoris'; Murimuth, p. 9: 'inordinata affectione dilexit'; *Lanercost*, p. 210: 'propter quamdam familiaritatem indebitam'; Trivet, p. 1: 'pro nimia familiaritate'; *Vita*, p. 15: 'Modum autem dilectionis rex noster habere non potuit'. For a comparative assessment of the chronicles of the reign, see Antonia Gransden, *Historical Writing in England*, ii (c.1307 to the early 16th cent.) (London, 1982), 1–55.

[9] *Flores*, iii. 229.

handsome lady and a very beautiful woman'.[10] But all this is more likely to have been just malicious gossip, no more trustworthy than the gratuitous assertion of the late Meaux chronicle that Edward indulged in the vice of sodomy 'excessively'.[11] To the more sedate author of the *Vita*, who was no admirer of either Edward or Gaveston, the love between the two was of the same kind as that of Jonathan for David, and of Achilles for Patroclus, but of greater intensity.[12] The *Vita* also says that, after Gaveston's murder, Edward spoke as David had done after the death of Jonathan, whose love David valued above the love of women.[13] Nowhere in the *Vita* is there any suggestion that anything improper of a physical nature ever took place between Edward and Gaveston.

Edward's attitude towards women does not appear to have been very different from that of other men of his time. Isabella bore him a son, the future Edward III, when she was 16, not an abnormally advanced age, even in the fourteenth century, for a woman to bear her first child; three other children were to follow.[14] Edward also had an illegitimate son, Adam.[15] All this is well authenticated in extant public records. So is the story that, on Easter Monday 1311, the king was heaved out of bed by Joan de Villers, Alice de la Leygrave (who had been Edward's second wet nurse), and other ladies of the queen's chamber.[16] Perhaps we should not attach too much importance to this episode, which simply illustrates what is known to have been an ancient custom, apparently connected with the commemoration of Christ's rising: on Easter Monday, any man found lying in bed by women could be lifted out by them and made to pay a ransom.[17] On at least three Easter Mondays, Edward I had been caught in that way

[10] *Ann. Paul.*, p. 262.

[11] *Melsa*, ii. 355.

[12] *Vita*, p. 15.

[13] Ibid., p. 30. See 2 Sam. 1: 26.

[14] *Brit. Chron.*, p. 39. For the date of Isabella's birth, see P. Doherty, 'The Date of the Birth of Isabella, Queen of England, 1308–1358', *BIHR* 48 (1975), 246–8.

[15] F. D. Blackley, 'Adam, the Bastard Son of Edward II', *BIHR* 37 (1964), 76–7. The argument that Edward may have been bisexual cannot be answered.

[16] Bodl. Lib. MS Tanner 197, fo. 54ᵛ: 'Johanne de Villar', Alicie de la Leygrave et aliis domicellis camere regine trahentibus regem de lecto suo die lune in crastino Pasche de dono ipsius regis per manus dicte Alicie recipientis denarios ibidem eodem die [i.e. *Berwick-upon-Tweed, 11 May 1311*], xl mar.'. On Joan de Villers and Alice de la Leygrave, see Johnstone, *Edw. of Carnarvon*, p. 9; *Isabella's Household Book*, p. xiv.

[17] Christina Hole, *Easter and its Customs* (London, 1961), pp. 52–3.

by ladies in the queen's service;[18] on one of these occasions, in Gascony in 1287, the ladies in question received a collective gift of £12 from the king's wardrobe.[19] Whatever Edward II may have thought of the custom, there is no reason to think that he was unduly put out by it, since in 1311 the ladies of Queen Isabella's chamber received from him as a pseudo-ransom the handsome gift of 40 marks, more than twice the amount paid by Edward I in 1287.[20] What is perhaps more relevant is that Edward II was treated by the ladies in the queen's service, one of whom, Alice de la Leygrave, had known him from infancy, in very much the same way as his father had been by their predecessors.

Finally, it is difficult to believe that Philip the Fair would have given away his 12-year-old daughter in marriage to a man whose ethics in love did not conform to the high standard which he expected of a son-in-law. When royal marriages were contemplated, it was normal practice for the character and habits of the prospective bride and groom to be thoroughly investigated.[21] That Philip might have been remiss in that respect is unthinkable, particularly if there were rumours that Edward and Gaveston were lovers. Although the marriage had been arranged almost ten years earlier as part of Boniface VIII's arbitration award of 27 June 1298, we can be sure that Philip would have refused to comply in 1308, if there had been by then any doubts about the intended bridegroom's moral character. He would in any case rather have forgotten an award made by a pope whom he had subsequently and slanderously accused of sodomy, a crime which he and his contemporaries seem to have regarded as one of the most hideous ones that could be committed by anybody; the same charge was to be levelled at the Templars at his instigation or at least with his approval.[22] The fact that Boniface had made his award not as pope but in his private capacity as Benedetto Gaetani made matters even worse. How could Philip have agreed to the celebration, in January 1308, of a marriage arranged by an alleged sodomite

---

[18] L. F. Salzman, *Edward I* (London, 1968), p. 189; *Records of the Wardrobe and Household, 1286–1289*, ed. B. F. Byerly and C. R. Byerly (HMSO, 1986), no. 980.

[19] Ibid., no. 980. [20] Bodl. Lib. MS Tanner 197, fo. 54ᵛ.

[21] Chaplais, *EMDP* I. i, nos. 60, 120, and nn.

[22] See Elizabeth A. R. Brown, *The Monarchy of Capetian France and Royal Ceremonial* (Variorum Collected Studies, cccxlv, 1991), ii. 290–1, and nn.; John Boswell, *Christianity, Social Tolerance, and Homosexuality* (Univ. of Chicago Press, 1980), pp. 296–7.

between his beloved daughter Isabella and Edward, if there had been the slightest suspicion that the bridegroom himself indulged in 'sinning against nature'?

Whatever reason the French king may have had only a few months later, in May 1308, for declaring Gaveston his enemy and, in effect, for blackmailing Edward into banishing him, as stated in a news-letter sent by an unknown writer to an unknown correspondent on the fourteenth of that month,[23] it is more likely to have been connected with politics than with morals or with the future of his daughter's marriage. Perhaps it was feared in Paris that Gaveston might have designs on Ponthieu, where, instead of Gascony, he had spent his first exile and which Edward had wanted to give him in 1306; or that Edward might still have plans for him in that county, a very sensitive region, not far from rebellious Flanders.[24] If the king of France had such fears, they were soon allayed: on 14 May, significantly the day on which the news-letter was sent, Edward granted to his wife the whole of Ponthieu and Montreuil and its revenues to cover all the expenses of her chamber, thus showing not only that he had no intention of giving the county to Gaveston, but also that he took Isabella's welfare very much to heart.[25] Philip also had other reasons for disliking Gaveston and his family. He was not the sort of person who would easily forget that Gaveston's father Arnaud had, a little more than a decade earlier, escaped from the French prison in which he was legitimately detained as a hostage on Edward I's behalf,[26] or that in 1297 Piers himself had served in Flanders with Edward I's expeditionary forces against the French.[27]

The mud-slinging efforts of late chroniclers have been so successful that they have made us overlook the significance of what may seem at first sight a very small point, which had been made by their more reliable predecessors, namely that Edward called Gaveston his brother. This is definitely stated by the *Vita*, the Chronicle of Lanercost, the *Annales Paulini*, the Chronicle of Walter of Guisborough,

---

[23] Maddicott, *Lancaster*, pp. 83, 335.

[24] According to Walter of Guisborough, Edward of Carnarvon asked his father to allow him to grant the county of Ponthieu to Gaveston [in 1306] (Guisborough, p. 382). Gaveston also spent his first exile in the county instead of going to Gascony as decreed at Lanercost on 26 Feb. 1307 (Hamilton, *Gaveston*, pp. 35–6).

[25] *Foedera*: R. II. i. 44; Maddicott, *Lancaster*, pp. 83–4, 335–6.

[26] Hamilton, *Gaveston*, p. 24.

[27] Ibid., p. 29.

as well as the *Polistorie* of Christ Church, Canterbury. The *Vita*, for example, says that, on Gaveston's return from Ireland in June 1309, the king went to meet him at Chester, where he received him with honour like his brother ('tamquam fratrem suum'). 'Indeed,' the author adds, 'he had always called him his brother.'[28] In August 1311, again according to the *Vita*, Edward told the barons that he would enforce the Ordinances, but they were to stop persecuting his brother Piers ('Verum a persecutione fratris mei Petri desistatis').[29] The *Annales Paulini* make the further point that it was because of his excessive love for Gaveston ('pre amore nimio') that Edward called him his brother.[30] According to the *Polistorie*, he already did so when he was only prince of Wales.[31] The Chronicle of Lanercost agrees, specifying that Edward called Gaveston his brother in public ('publice').[32] This additional point is confirmed by the wording of a privy seal writ of 5 July 1308, addressed to Walter Reynolds, bishop elect of Worcester, treasurer. The writ, which has survived in a contemporary exchequer enrolment, tells Reynolds:

We are sending you enclosed herein a letter which our dear brother and faithful Peres de Gaveston', earl of Cornwall, has sent us on behalf of Elys Scarlet, and we order you that, after examining the said letter, you take, regarding the said Elys and the matters mentioned therein, whatever suitable action needs to be taken.[33]

The words 'our dear brother and faithful' (*nostre cher frere et feal*) were precisely those which the king used when he wrote or referred to his true half-brothers Thomas of Brotherton and Edmund of Woodstock.[34] In an original privy seal writ issued on the same day, 5 July 1308, and connected with the same matter, Edward referred to Gaveston as 'nostre feal et loial'.[35] Since Gaveston had sailed to Ireland to begin

---

[28] *Vita*, p. 7. [29] Ibid., p. 17. [30] *Ann. Paul.*, p. 259; see also p. 273.
[31] BL MS Harl. 636, fo. 232[r]. [32] *Lanercost*, p. 210.
[33] The writ (cited in Conway Davies, *Baron. Opp.*, p. 84 n. 14), PRO E 159/81, m. 34d, reads as follows: 'Edward par la grace de Dieu etc. al honurable pere en Dieu W. par la meisme grace eslit de Wyrecestre conferme, nostre tresorier, saluz. Nous vous enveoms une[s] lettres encloses dedeinz cestes, qe nostre cher frere et feal Peres de Gavaston', counte de Cornwall', nous ad envees por Elys Scarlet, et vous mandoms qe, veues les dites lettres, facez faire pur le dit Elys endroyt des bosoignes qe y sount contenues ceo qe vous verrez qe face a faire en bone manere. Done souz nostre prive seal a Wodestok' le v jour de juyl, lan de nostre regne primere.'
[34] Chaplais, *EMDP* I. i. 104, 109 n. 199; Chaplais, *ERD*, pl. 12 (in the transcription, the word *frere* is omitted); *Parl. Writs*, II. ii. 539 and app. p. 158.
[35] PRO C 81/60/258; *Cal. Chanc. War.* i. 276.

his second exile exactly one week before the issue of the two writs, the exceptional use of the word *frere* in one and of *loial* in the other can without doubt be attributed to Edward himself, who thus wished to stress that he completely rejected the charge of treason to the king and to his realm which the barons had brought against the Gascon in order to have him exiled.[36] Normally, royal official documents referred to Gaveston as 'nostre cher et foial' in French and 'dilectus et fidelis noster' in Latin, the words used as a rule for any of the king's lieges.[37]

It could be argued that, by calling Gaveston his brother, Edward merely showed that he had a special affection for him. That it was more than a figure of speech, however, is suggested by the *Vita* and the *Annales Paulini*. In one passage, the author of the *Vita* explains what a momentous decision it had been for the earls to order the murder of Gaveston: 'They have killed a great earl whom the king had adopted as brother' (*Occiderunt enim magnum comitem quem rex adoptaverat in fratrem*).[38] On one occasion, the author of the *Annales Paulini* also describes Gaveston as the king's adoptive brother, when he remarks that in 1308 the king could not bring himself to send into exile the person of Piers Gaveston, his adoptive brother ('adoptivi fratris sui').[39] What Edward II's biographer and the annalist of St Paul's meant was that Edward and Gaveston, who were not related by blood, had contracted an artificial bond of fraternity, as other men had done from ancient times. Only one chronicle, the anonymous 'Chronicle of the Civil Wars of Edward II',[40] refers specifically to such a bond, a compact of brotherhood ('fraternitatis fedus'), which would have been concluded between Edward of Carnarvon and Gaveston in the last decade of Edward I's reign, some time after Gaveston was received in the royal household as a squire (*armiger*).[41] The relevant passage of the chronicle tells us that, when he cast his eyes on Gaveston, 'the king's son felt so much love for him that he entered into a compact of brotherhood with him and chose and

---

[36] Richardson and Sayles, *The Governance of Mediaeval England*, p. 468.
[37] See e.g. PRO C 81/60/210, 215, 246, 249, 258, etc.
[38] *Vita*, p. 28.   [39] *Ann. Paul.*, p. 263.
[40] BL MS Cotton Cleopatra D ix, fos. 86ʳ–88ʳ (George L. Haskins, 'A Chronicle of the Civil Wars of Edward II', *Speculum*, 14 (1939), 73–81).
[41] The word *armiger* is also applied to Gaveston in the *Vita*, p. 14. Saul had also made David his *armiger* (1 Sam. 16: 21).

decided to tie himself to him, against all mortals, in an unbreakable bond of affection'.[42] The chronicle does not say whether the compact was written down, but if any document or documents were drawn up, it is probable that, on the occasion of the Lanercost oaths of 26 February 1307, Edward I would have insisted on their destruction.[43]

A biblical precedent: Jonathan and David

From the east and from the west, explicit or implicit references to compacts of brotherhood are not lacking. The numerous allusions made in the Bible to the agreement entered into by Jonathan with David deserve to be cited as perhaps the earliest among them (1 Sam. 18: 3: 'inierunt autem Jonathan et David foedus');[44] although the Bible does not specify what kind of agreement it was, the fact that, on one occasion, in his lament upon Jonathan, David called him his brother (2 Sam. 1: 26: 'Doleo super te, frater mi Jonathan') suggests, to say the least, that the agreement in question was a compact of adoptive brotherhood. The agreement, which was to last for ever between the two men and their descendants, had been strengthened by mutual oaths;[45] Jonathan had bound himself further to David by taking off his tunic and other garments as well as his sword, bow, and belt, and giving them to him.[46] It was in the court of his father, King Saul, that Jonathan had made the acquaintance of David, who had been retained by Saul as musician and *armiger*.[47] When, some time later, the king heard of the compact made by Jonathan with David, he became very angry, warning his son that he could expect nothing but disaster for himself and for the kingdom of Israel as long as David lived:

You son of a perverse and rebellious woman! Do I not know that you have sided with the son of Jesse to your own shame and to the shame of the mother

---

[42] BL MS Cotton Cleopatra D ix, fo. 86ʳ (*Speculum*, 14 (1939), 75, where the word *firmitatis* should be corrected to *fraternitatis*): 'Quem [sc. Gaveston] filius regis intuens, in eum tantum protinus amorem iniecit quod cum eo fraternitatis fedus iniit, et pre ceteris mortalibus indissolubile dileccionis vinculum secum elegit et firm[i]ter disposuit innodare.' Compare Trokelowe, p. 64: 'spretis magnatum terre liberis, sibi soli in tantum adhesit quod nec patris sui preceptum aut suasio magnatum eos ab invicem usque ad mortem animo saltem potuit separare'. [43] For the Lanercost ceremony, see *Foedera*: R. I. ii. 1010.
[44] See also 1 Sam. 20: 8, 16, 42; 22: 8; 23: 18. [45] 1 Sam. 20: 42.
[46] 1 Sam. 18: 4. [47] 1 Sam. 16: 21–3.

who bore you? As long as the son of Jesse lives on this earth, neither you nor your kingdom will be established.[48]

David had to be killed; he survived, mostly thanks to Jonathan's unwavering support. It was apparently while he was hiding from Saul that, according to the Bible, David was told by Jonathan: 'You shall be king over Israel and I will be second to you' (1 Sam. 23: 17: 'et tu regnabis super Israhel et ego ero tibi secundus'). These words were followed by the statement that both made an agreement before the Lord (1 Sam. 23: 18: 'percussit igitur uterque foedus coram Domino'), perhaps a mere renewal of the compact which they had made earlier.

Continental and English cases of adoptive brotherhood in the eleventh and twelfth centuries

In so far as the Middle Ages are concerned, references to compacts of adoptive brotherhood occur in both continental and English chronicles. In the 1070s, according to Gaufredus Malaterra, the Saracen Ibrahim from Castrogiovanni in Sicily concluded an agreement ('foedus inierat') with Serlo, son of Serlo of Hauteville, each taking the other as adoptive brother ('adoptivum fratrem') by pulling his ear in the Muslim fashion. Thus Ibrahim hoped to put Serlo off his guard and bring about his death.[49] For the mid-twelfth century, Hugo Falcandus cites the compact of brotherly fellowship ('fraterne fedus societatis') which, following the Sicilian custom, the grand admiral Maio had contracted with the archbishop of Palermo; they had sworn to assist one another in every way and to be of one mind, will, and counsel in good as well as bad fortune; whoever harmed either of them would incur the enmity of both.[50] In these two Sicilian examples two partners only were involved, and each of them adopted the other as brother. In a third case, which comes from the *Gesta Normannorum*

---

[48] 1 Sam. 20: 30–1: 'Fili mulieris virum ultro rapientis, numquid ignoro quia diligis filium Isai in confusionem tuam et in confusionem ignominiosae matris tuae? Omnibus enim diebus quibus filius Isai vixerit super terram, non stabilieris tu neque regnum tuum.' The translation is taken from *The Holy Bible, New International Version* (2nd imp., London, 1988), pp. 296–7.

[49] Du Cange, 'Des adoptions d'honneur en frère, et, par occasion, des frères d'armes', *Dissertations sur l'histoire de Saint Louys*, XXI (*Glossarium mediae et infimae latinitatis*, x (1887), 67); *Gaufredi Malaterre . . . Historia Sicula*, bk. ii, ch. 46 (L. A. Muratori, *Rerum Italicarum Scriptores*, V. i (Bologna, 1927), 53).

[50] Du Cange, 'Des adoptions d'honneur en frère' (*Glossarium*, x. 68); Keen, 'Brotherhood in Arms', pp. 3–4.

ducum of William of Jumièges, Duke Robert I of Normandy (1027–35) is said to have adopted as brothers his two cousins Edward and Alfred, Æthelred II's sons, who were at the time exiles in Normandy ('summi nexu amoris tanquam fratres sibi eos adoptaverit').[51] Although this adoption, like any other, must have resulted in reciprocal obligations, the chronicler's wording suggests that it was one-sided, perhaps because of the inequality of status between Duke Robert, an actual ruler, and the athelings Edward and Alfred, who, besides being under age, were only potential rulers.

English chronicles written between 1100 and 1150 also mention or imply four instances of the practice of adoptive brotherhood in England. The earliest is a reference allegedly made *c.*656 by Wulfhere, king of Mercia, to Oswiu, king of Northumbria and overlord of the southern kingdoms, as his 'pledged brother' (*wed broðer*), implying therefore an improbable agreement of brotherhood between them. The reference occurs only in version E of the Anglo-Saxon Chronicle, in a passage which was interpolated at Peterborough in the first quarter of the twelfth century, at about the same time as the charter of 664 attributed to Wulfhere in favour of Medeshamstede was forged.[52] Its only interest is to confirm that the expression *wed broðer* had become the accepted Old-English equivalent of the Latin *frater adoptivus* by the time the interpolation was made.

The first apparently trustworthy evidence for adoptive brotherhood in England consists of the chroniclers' account of the treaty of Alney concluded between Cnut and Edmund Ironside in 1016. It was more than a treaty of peace: all versions of the Anglo-Saxon Chronicle except D say that it was a friendship agreement strengthened by pledge and oaths, while Florence of Worcester speaks of peace, friendship, and brotherhood, also confirmed by pledge and oaths ('pace, amicitia, fraternitate, et pacto et sacramentis confirmata'), and version D of the Chronicle states instead that Cnut and Edmund became partners and pledged brothers ('feolagan and wed broðra').[53] According to Henry of Huntingdon, the agreement was made at the suggestion of Cnut, who (in a speech no doubt imaginary) is supposed

---

[51] Guillaume de Jumièges, *Gesta Normannorum ducum*, ed. Jean Marx (Société de l'histoire de Normandie, Rouen, 1914), p. 109. I owe this reference to the kindness of Dr M. K. Lawson.

[52] *Two of the Saxon Chronicles Parallel*, ed. Plummer, i. 29; ii. 25–6.

[53] Ibid. i. 152–3; Florence of Worcester, i. 178.

to have said to Edmund: 'Let us be adoptive brothers (*fratres adoptivi*) and let us divide the kingdom'.[54] William of Malmesbury adds that, later in the year, after Edmund had died, Cnut referred to him on one occasion as 'frater mihi federatus', which was another way of saying that they were adoptive brothers.[55]

As the result of the treaty of Alney, the English kingdom was divided into two: Cnut acquired Mercia (or 'the North') as king, and Edmund retained Wessex also as king. It had also been agreed that, whichever of them died first, the survivor was to be the sole king of all England.[56] From Cnut's point of view, this was a most satisfactory arrangement, which gave him the appearance of magnanimity and at the same time assured him of the lawful and (hopefully) peaceful possession of the whole of England, should his adoptive brother Edmund conveniently die first, as in fact he did. All the natural heirs of Edmund had by treaty been eliminated from the succession to the throne. There seems to be no doubt that the treaty of Alney was essentially, as the chronicles claim or imply, an agreement of adoptive brotherhood, although it had wider implications than other known compacts of this type. It may be significant that, according to Florence of Worcester, Cnut and Edmund Ironside exchanged weapons and clothes before taking their leave of one another at Alney, an interesting detail which reminds us of Jonathan handing over to David his own weapons and clothes.[57] In the case of Jonathan and David, it was a one-sided, unreciprocated gift, perhaps because David was at the time of lower status than Jonathan, whereas the two royal partners at Alney were equal.

Within less than six weeks of his compact with Cnut, Edmund died (30 November 1016). The Anglo-Saxon Chronicle and Florence of Worcester simply note without any comment that Edmund passed away on the feast of St Andrew.[58] That he might have died from anything but natural causes does not seem to have occurred to either of them. To some of the contemporaries who were aware of the

---

[54] Henry of Huntingdon, p. 185.   [55] William of Malmesbury, *Gesta Regum*, i. 219.

[56] Henry of Huntingdon, p. 185; William of Malmesbury, *Gesta Regum*, i. 217; F. Barlow, *Edward the Confessor* (London, 1970), p. 36 n. 2; compare p. 48 n. 2; *Two of the Saxon Chronicles Parallel*, ed. Plummer, ii. 199.

[57] Florence of Worcester, i. 178–9; compare 1 Sam. 18: 4.

[58] *Two of the Saxon Chronicles Parallel*, ed. Plummer, i. 153; ii. 199; Florence of Worcester, i. 179.

provisions of the Alney agreement, however, Edmund's premature demise may have given food for thought. A later writer would almost certainly have suspected foul play. Writing a hundred years or so after the event, William of Malmesbury remarks that the cause of death was uncertain ('ambiguum quo casu extinctus'). He goes on to say that, according to tradition, Edmund had been the victim of a vile murder engineered by Eadric Streona, ealdorman of Mercia.[59] For Henry of Huntingdon, who appears to have been in no doubt that it was murder, the guilty man was also Eadric, who unwisely boasted about it to Cnut, greeting him with the words: 'Ave, rex solus'.[60] Unlike some Scandinavian authors,[61] both William of Malmesbury and Henry of Huntingdon exonerate Cnut from blame, making him avenge his adoptive brother's death by having Eadric executed.[62]

The agreement of Alney had brought a foreign war to a close. The next English compact of adoptive brotherhood to which we have a reference was intended to halt what Sir Frank Stenton called 'the most remarkable private feud in English history'.[63] In 1016, while he was on his way to make peace with King Cnut and travelling in Cnut's safe conduct, Uhtred, earl of Northumbria, was killed by some of the king's men at the instigation of Thurbrand the Hold. Soon afterwards Thurbrand was in turn murdered by Ealdred, son of Uhtred and now earl of Northumbria. In due course, through the mediation of common friends, peace was restored between the two sides. Carl, son of Thurbrand, and Ealdred became sworn brothers ('fratres adjurati'). They were to go to Rome together, but stormy seas made them abandon the pilgrimage. After staying in Carl's house, where he had been lavishly entertained, the unsuspecting Ealdred was murdered by his host in a nearby forest as he was escorted back by him out of feigned deference.[64] Although the two men are said to have become

---

[59] William of Malmesbury, *Gesta Regum*, i. 217, 219.

[60] Henry of Huntingdon, p. 186.

[61] E. A. Freeman, *The History of the Norman Conquest*, i (1st edn. 1867), p. 439 n. 1; (3rd edn. 1877), p. 715. In his 3rd edn., Freeman studies the evidence regarding Edmund's death in considerable detail (pp. 711–17); I am indebted to Mr James Campbell for bringing this to my attention.

[62] Henry of Huntingdon, p. 186; William of Malmesbury, *Gesta Regum*, i. 219.

[63] F. Stenton, *Anglo-Saxon England* (2nd edn. Oxford, 1947), p. 384 n. 1.

[64] Simeon of Durham, *Opera*, ed. T. Arnold, i (RS, 1882), 219. For another similar feud, this time in Normandy, see *The Ecclesiastical History of Orderic Vitalis*, ed. Marjorie Chibnall, ii (Oxford Medieval Texts, 2nd edn. 1990), 14.

sworn brothers out of love ('in amorem alterutrum sunt adunati'),[65] it
is probable that Carl had resorted to the device of adoptive
brotherhood in order to delude Ealdred into a sense of false security.
Later in the century, as we have seen, the Saracen Ibrahim was to use
the same method with equal success in his dealings with Serlo in
Sicily.

All our information on the feud between Uhtred and Thurbrand
and their respective descendants comes from a northern source, the
so-called *De obsessione Dunelmi*. From another northern source, the
Historia regum of Simeon of Durham, we learn that in 1061 Malcolm
III, king of Scots, laid waste [Northumbria], the earldom of Earl
Tostig, his sworn brother ('sui conjurati fratris'),[66] a further instance
of a compact of adoptive brotherhood which, for one of the brothers,
had not come up to expectation.

Neither in the case of Ealdred and Carl nor in that of Malcolm and
Tostig do we know what was entailed in the agreement between the
two adoptive brothers. In both cases the partners are described as
'sworn brothers', a common designation for adoptive brothers of all
types, including brothers-in-arms (*frere d'armes*, or *frere adoptif et
d'armes*, or *freres et compaignons d'armes*, in French; *socii in armis*, in
Latin).[67] The association known as brotherhood-in-arms, widespread
in the late-fourteenth and fifteenth centuries, especially, it seems,
among young men of knightly or lesser rank about to go to war, did
not attract much attention from chroniclers or biographers of any date
unless, exceptionally, those involved were of high standing or had
achieved notoriety or fame. This kind of brotherhood, however, had
by the fifteenth century 'a respectable antiquity';[68] it may have been
practised as early as 1100, the approximate date of composition of the
Chanson de Roland. The poem's two main heroes Roland and Olivier
normally refer to one another as 'companion' ('cumpainz'), and
Roland calls Olivier 'frere' on four occasions and 'compaign frere'
once, a combination of modes of address which, two centuries or so

---

[65] Simeon of Durham, *Opera*, i. 219.
[66] Ibid. ii. 174-5.
[67] Philippe Contamine, *Guerre, état et société à la fin du Moyen Age* (Paris, 1972), p. 483 nn.
141-2; Keen, 'Brotherhood in Arms', pp. 3, 7 n. 28, 9; P. C. Timbal, *La Guerre de Cent ans vue à
travers les registres du Parlement (1337-69)* (Paris, 1961), p. 323.
[68] K. B. McFarlane, 'A Business-Partnership in War and Administration, 1421-1445', *EHR*
78 (1963), 291.

I. Extracts in reduced size from Edward II's original charter granting the earldom of Cornwall to Gaveston (PRO E41/460; 6 Aug. 1307):
(*a*) upper left-hand corner
(*b*) middle of upper portion

(*a*)

(*b*)

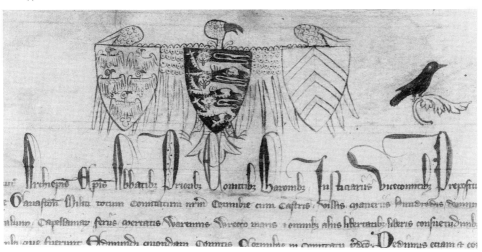

II. Substitute Great Seal Prototype of Henry III
(BL Seals li. 18 and 19; casts; ? before 1259). *Actual size.*

III. Substitute Great Seal of Henry III (Canterbury Cathedral Archives, Charta antiqua C. 78; 27 Feb. 1264). *Actual size.*

IV. Great Seal of absence of Edward II (Oxford, Oriel
College Archives, DL 9/A. 10; 16 June 1320).
Actual size.

later, would almost certainly have denoted brotherhood-in-arms.[69] Also, when Olivier, mortally wounded and losing his eyesight, strikes Roland on the head accidentally, the latter gently rebukes him, asking whether he had struck him on purpose (which he should not have done), because he had not defied him.[70] This additional point fits in well with what we know of the rules which governed relations between brothers-in-arms: amongst other things, the brothers promised to be loyal to one another, which precluded, of course, any unprovoked attack of one on the other unless it had been preceded by a defiance.[71]

The duties and rights attached to brotherhood-in-arms may have varied somewhat over the years and, in a given period, from one pair of brothers to the next. But the credit side of the association was obviously attractive enough to induce a young man with a military career in mind to become the companion and sworn brother of another man of his own age for whom he felt friendship and affection. It would give him not only a welcome protection against some of the risks involved in going to war, but also a guarantee of substantial profits. The few examples of written compacts still extant and what may be gleaned from romances of chivalry give us some details on the nature of the relationship. The two partners promised to give one another assistance in every respect against all men except those to whom they were bound by ties of allegiance. If either of them was captured by an enemy, his partner would pay his ransom himself or at least contribute towards it and arrange for the rest of the money to be found. Gains of war such as ransoms or booty were to be shared equally between the two brothers. Should one of them die, the survivor would have his partner's share in all their war gains in addition to his own half, but a proportion was to be assigned as a dower to the dead man's widow and provision made for the sustenance and education of his children. Faithful execution of the compact was normally guaranteed by oaths sworn personally by the two brothers, who might also take communion together, sometimes sharing the same host.[72] So personal was their relationship that they

---

[69] *La Chanson de Roland*, ed. F. Whitehead (Oxford, 1968): *cumpainz* and variants: lines 1006, 1020, 1059, 1113, 1146, 1546, 1716, 1976, etc.; *frere*: lines 1376, 1395, 1698, 1866; *compaign frere*: 1456.　　　　　　　　　　　　　　　　　　　　[70] Ibid., lines 2000–2.
[71] Keen, 'Brotherhood in Arms', p. 11.
[72] Ibid., pp. 1–17, *passim*; McFarlane in *EHR* 78 (1963), 290, 309–10.

might exchange weapons and clothes or bear the same heraldic device on their arms.[73]

Were Edward and Gaveston brothers-in-arms?

If the *fraternitatis fedus* which Edward of Carnarvon and Piers Gaveston concluded some time between 1297 and 1307 was a compact of brotherhood-in-arms, as it may well have been, it would explain why, in the articles of 1308, Edward, now king, is said to have undertaken 'to support Gaveston against everyone on all points' (*dominus rex predictum Petrum contra omnes in omnibus articulis manutenere vult*);[74] this is exactly the phraseology which we might have expected Edward as prince to use in a brotherhood compact with Gaveston; he would have added, of course, a clause reserving his allegiance to his father Edward I, but by 1308 this saving clause had been made obsolete by the old king's death and the younger Edward's own accession. A likely date for the compact would seem to be some time in 1300 or early in 1301, two important years in the life of both Edward of Carnarvon and Gaveston: it was during that period that Edward became prince of Wales, that Piers Gaveston was transferred from the household of Edward I to that of his son, and that both young men became involved together for the first time in Edward I's Scottish wars.[75] If Edward, although no coward, lacked enthusiasm for military pursuits, as he apparently did, having a sworn brother and companion who excelled in them would have been a great comfort.

Whatever the detailed terms of the compact may have been, the very idea of a brotherhood agreement, based on the principle of sharing alike, between the heir to the throne and a Gascon squire, cannot have been anything but distressing to the king and distasteful to the great men of the kingdom. What might happen when the heir to the throne eventually became king did not bear thinking about. Perhaps for a time Edward and Gaveston kept their agreement to themselves, but their secret was bound to come out sooner or later. This may have happened late in 1306, on the occasion of what was

---

[73] Keen, 'Brotherhood in Arms', p. 13; Chaucer, *The Knight's Tale*, line 154; Du Cange, 'Des adoptions d'honneur en frère' (*Glossarium*, x. 69).

[74] *Bridlington*, p. 34; Richardson and Sayles, *The Governance of Mediaeval England*, p. 468.

[75] Johnstone, *Edw. of Carnarvon*, pp. 43, 75; Hamilton, *Gaveston*, pp. 29–30.

possibly Edward's first effort to raise the status of his adoptive brother. For a compact of adoptive brotherhood to be reasonably successful, the partners had to be of comparable rank and prospects. This certainly was not the case, nor could it ever be, in so far as Edward and Gaveston were concerned. In 1301 Gaveston was still a *scutifer*, whereas Edward was prince of Wales and enjoyed a considerable land endowment consisting, on this side of the Channel, not only of Wales, but also of the earldom of Chester; in addition, on the Continent, he had in 1290, on the death of his mother Eleanor of Castile, inherited the county of Ponthieu.[76] Gaveston's knighting, on Thursday, 26 May 1306, four days after the prince of Wales had himself been knighted by his father on Whit Sunday, 22 May, did not in reality alter the discrepancy between their respective situations.[77] Indeed by then the gap had even widened, as in the meantime Edward had been granted by his father the duchy of Guyenne and the lands associated with it in the south-west of France (7 April 1306).[78]

It was, it seems, towards the end of 1306 that the prince asked Edward I to allow him to grant the county of Ponthieu to Gaveston. The old king's reaction, as recounted by Walter of Guisborough, is well known: his anger and verbal abuse, followed by a physical assault on the prince. 'You base-born whoreson', Edward is supposed to have said to his son, 'do you want to give away lands now, you who never gained any? As the Lord lives, if it were not for fear of breaking up the kingdom, you should never enjoy your inheritance.'[79] We know that Edward I was irascible, increasingly so as he grew older. But the words which Guisborough places in his mouth are so reminiscent of those which the Vulgate attributes to Saul in the angry scene in which he tells his son Jonathan that he is aware of his attachment to David that we may wonder whether they really were Edward's

[76] Johnstone, *Edw. of Carnarvon*, pp. 42 n. 5, 55–65.
[77] For the knighting of Edward, see ibid., pp. 107–8; Bodl. Lib. MS Lat. Hist. c. 4 (R), m. 5, under date of Whit Sunday, 22 May: 'Memorandum quod isto die dominico princeps factus fuit miles et ideo majores fuerunt expense per ebdomadam sequentem.' Gaveston was not knighted on the same day as Edward, but four days later; see Bodl. Lib. MS Lat. Hist. c. 4 (R), m. 5, under date of Thursday, 26 May: 'Isto die jovis factus fuit Petrus de Gavaston' miles et alii diversi in comitiva sua et fuerunt in prandio fere omnes magnates regni.'
[78] Johnstone, *Edw. of Carnarvon*, p. 109.
[79] Guisborough, p. 382: 'Fili meretricis male generate, vis tu modo terras dare qui nuncquam aliquas impetrasti? Viuit dominus, nisi esset timor dispersionis regni, nuncquam gauderes hereditate tua'; Johnstone, *Edw. of Carnarvon*, p. 123.

ipsissima verba.[80] The episode itself, however, may have occurred. Perhaps it was responsible, at least partly, for Edward I's decision to sever for an indefinite period all ties between his son and Gaveston. At a ceremony held at Lanercost on Sunday, 26 February 1307, solemn oaths on the body of Christ and on the royal relics, including the *Crux natans*, were sworn by Gaveston that he would leave England from Dover to go to Gascony via Wissant five weeks after Easter, not to return without the king's recall or licence, and by the prince that he would not receive or retain the Gascon without the king's permission.[81] The official record of the ceremony, on the dorse of the Close Roll, and the Chronicle of John de Trokelowe state that the king had ordered Gaveston's exile 'for certain reasons'.[82] The annalist of St Paul's is more specific: according to him, Edward I imagined that, after his death, the excessive love of his son for Gaveston might create numerous problems for the kingdom.[83] It might indeed, if the brotherhood compact which the two young men had contracted and probably confirmed by oaths was allowed to stand. Could the brotherhood be dissolved by claiming that the oaths taken by the two partners were illicit as contrary to the general good of the country? At least its effects could be nullified if Gaveston was exiled for life, as some chroniclers claim that he was: 'perpetuo' according to one, 'eternaliter' according to a second, 'absque aliqua gracia seu spe in posterum redeundi' according to a third.[84] The official record, however, says otherwise: Gaveston was to remain in exile as long as the king did not recall him or allow him to return.[85] The wording of the document leaves us in no doubt that the king in question was meant to be the reigning one at the time of the ceremony, that is to say Edward I, for the eventuality of whose death no provision was made. When that death occurred, the prince of Wales and Gaveston would be justified in regarding themselves as released from their oaths, which in any case had been taken under duress and were therefore invalid.

---

[80] Compare 1 Sam. 20: 30–1. See Johnstone, *Edw. of Carnarvon*, p. 123; Hamilton, *Gaveston*, pp. 34–5.   [81] *Foedera*: R. I. ii. 1010.

[82] Ibid.: 'par acunes resons'; Trokelowe, p. 64: 'certis de causis'.

[83] *Ann. Paul.*, p. 255.

[84] Guisborough, p. 383: 'perpetuo'; Trokelowe, p. 64: 'eternaliter'; BL MS Cotton Cleopatra D ix, fo. 86ʳ (*Speculum*, 14 (1939), 75): 'absque aliqua gracia seu spe in posterum redeundi'.

[85] *Foedera*: R. I. ii. 1010.

2

ENGLAND'S SECOND KING?

Gaveston's return from Ponthieu

EDWARD I died at Burgh-by-Sands near Carlisle at three o'clock in the afternoon (*hora nona*) of 7 July 1307.[1] The first news of his father's death reached the prince on 11 July, on which day he was in or near London.[2] It had been brought to him by express messengers (*nuncii festini*),[3] who had covered the distance from Burgh-by-Sands to London (approximately 310 miles) in four days at the most, obviously with the help of relays of horses. Master Ralph Baldock, bishop of London and Edward I's last chancellor, who at the time was also in London with the royal chancery, heard the news probably on the same day as the prince and from the same source. Whoever the messengers may have been, perhaps couriers of the royal household, or merchants, their message is likely to have been a purely oral one, unsupported by letters of credence from anyone in authority. This is probably why Baldock did not give full credence to the news, treating it instead as a rumour until it was officially confirmed on 25 July. Until that date he continued to seal 'writs of course' (*brevia de cursu*) with Edward I's great seal by the advice of the king's council in London, which had been afforced from 11 July by the prince's chancellor, William of Blyborough, and by the keeper of his wardrobe, Walter Reynolds.[4] The adjunction of these two officials of the prince to the king's council is a strong indication that, as early as

---

[1] *Foedera*: R. I. ii. 1018; *Ann. Paul.*, p. 256; Guisborough, p. 379.
[2] PRO E 101/373/15, fo. 43ᵛ: 'ab xj die julii, quo die primo constitit principi de morte regis, patris sui'.   [3] *Lanercost*, p. 207.
[4] *Foedera*: R. I. ii. 1018; PRO E 101/373/15, fo. 43ᵛ.

11 July, the news of the king's death was regarded in London as reliable enough, at least by the prince of Wales. The latter seems to have left forthwith for the north, reaching Carlisle on 18 July.[5]

Once Edward I had died, Gaveston's return from exile need not have surprised anyone. What was unexpected was the almost indecent haste with which the new king recalled his adoptive brother, not even waiting until his father had been laid to rest, as the Chronicle of Walter of Guisborough put it.[6] An addition to the same chronicle goes further still, claiming that Gaveston's recall was the first action taken by Edward of Carnarvon after his accession.[7] This is echoed in the 'Chronicle of the Civil Wars of Edward II', which says that no sooner had Edward assumed the title of king than he recalled Gaveston.[8] These allegations should obviously not be taken too literally. What is virtually certain is that, however eager Edward may have been to see Gaveston back in England, he would not have dared to make arrangements for his return until he had received the first news of his father's death. We may therefore regard 11 July as the earliest possible date for the dispatch of a letter of recall from Edward to Gaveston. Ponthieu, of course, where Gaveston had remained throughout his exile instead of spending it in Gascony as had been ordained at Lanercost on 26 February 1307,[9] was conveniently close to England, but even an express messenger in ideal weather conditions could not have made the journey from London to Crécy via Dover and Wissant in less than three days, and the return trip would have taken a minimum of six days.[10] If a letter of recall was sent to Gaveston on 11 July, his reply could not have reached London before the seventeenth at the earliest. For this reason the presence in London on 16 July of a sick servant of Gaveston, Richard Dragon, is unlikely

[5] *Lanercost*, p. 207.

[6] Guisborough, p. 383.

[7] Ibid., p. 380.

[8] *Speculum*, 14 (1939), 75.

[9] *Foedera*: R. I. ii. 1010; Johnstone, *Edw. of Carnarvon*, pp. 71, 124–5; Hamilton, *Gaveston*, pp. 35–6.

[10] On a royal mission from London to Lyons in 1305, John de Benstede, who travelled at an average speed, was in London on Saturday, 23 Oct., Newington (Kent) on Sunday 24th, Dover on Monday 25th, Wissant on Tuesday 26th, Boulogne-sur-Mer on Wednesday 27th, and Crécy on Thursday 28th; next day he was in Amiens; on his way back, it also took him six days to travel from Amiens to London via Saint-Riquier, Montreuil-sur-Mer, Wissant, Dover, and Canterbury (PRO E 101/309/10). An express messenger would, of course, have travelled faster, perhaps in half the time.

to have been connected with his master's recall.[11] It may be worth noting, however, that during the week which began on 16 July messengers were unusually active between London and Ponthieu. On Sunday 16th Thomas de Chilham left London for Crécy with letters from 'the treasurer', that is to say Walter Reynolds, treasurer of the wardrobe.[12] Next day another messenger, John de Moleseye, also took letters from the treasurer to Ponthieu *pro negociis regis*.[13] Unlike the missions of Chilham and Moleseye, which, it could be argued, may have had nothing to do with Gaveston's recall, that of a third messenger almost certainly did: on Wednesday 19th Robert de Wokingham brought from somewhere between London and Carlisle to the London house of Walter Reynolds royal letters addressed to Gaveston.[14] This does not necessarily mean that Gaveston had already arrived in London by 19 July; the king's letters may have been taken to the house of Reynolds either to await Gaveston's arrival there or, more probably, so that Reynolds could forward them to Ponthieu. Since on the previous day, Tuesday 18th, Alan of Cornwall, a servant of Gaveston, was about to leave London, where he had arrived from Ponthieu, to go to the king *versus Scociam*, it is unlikely that his master had already returned to England.[15]

The royal letters brought to London by Robert de Wokingham on 19 July may have been Gaveston's letters of recall. Perhaps one may speculate further and suggest that it was Gaveston's reply which was brought from Ponthieu by his servant Robert le Somnour, who on 24 August received in London as a royal gift 6s. 8d. to buy himself a tunic.[16] This was a generous gift, representing exactly the half-yearly clothing allowance of a royal *nuncius*,[17] but a belated one, since between his arrival in London from Ponthieu and 24 August Robert

---

[11] PRO E 101/373/15, fo. 21ʳ (Hamilton, *Gaveston*, p. 139 n. 1): 'Ricardo Dragon, garcioni domini P. de Gavaston', infirmato apud Lond', de dono domini regis nomine sustentacionis sue in eadem infirmitate ibidem, per manus proprias apud Lond' xvj die julii, v s.'

[12] PRO E 101/373/15, fo. 25ʳ.   [13] Ibid.

[14] Ibid., fo. 23ʳ: 'xix die julii, Roberto de Wokingham, deferenti litteras regis domino P. de Gavaston' usque Lond' ad domum domini W. Reginaldi, pro expensis suis, iiij s. vj d.'

[15] Ibid., fo. 25ʳ (Hamilton, *Gaveston*, p. 139 n. 1).

[16] PRO E 101/373/15, fo. 21ᵛ: 'xxiiijᵗᵒ die augusti, Roberto le Somenour, garcioni domini P. de Gavaston', venienti ad regem de partibus Pontivi cum litteris domini sui, de dono regis ad unam tunicam sibi emendam, per manus proprias ibidem [sc. London'] eodem die, vj s. viij d.'

[17] Mary C. Hill, *The King's Messengers, 1199–1377* (London, 1961), p. 24.

had had time to take his master's letter to the king in Scotland and make his way back to London.[18] He may have arrived in London from Ponthieu with Gaveston's letter some time in the first week in August.[19]

It has proved impossible to establish the exact date of Gaveston's return to England. What we can say, however, is that it took place between 6 and 13 August. The first of these two dates is that of the royal charter granting the earldom of Cornwall to Gaveston,[20] which grant was made in the beneficiary's absence and without his knowledge ('sibi absenti et ignoranti'), or so the king claimed in letters addressed to the pope and to the king of France on 16 June 1308.[21] The second date, 13 August, is that of the payment of 16s., of the king's gift, to Robert de Rufford, yeoman of Gaveston, who had come from Ponthieu to London in his master's retinue and had been wounded during the journey.[22] Gaveston does not seem to have spent any appreciable length of time in London, but he pursued his journey towards Carlisle, where bread, beer, hay, oats, and wax were bought in August 'on Piers Gaveston's arrival there from abroad' ('in adventu domini Petri de Gavaston' ibidem de partibus transmarinis').[23] From Carlisle he went on to Scotland. It was presumably in anticipation of Gaveston's imminent arrival there that Geoffrey of Nottingham supplied some lengths of green and indigo silk 'to make arms [in the heraldic sense] therewith for the use of the earl of Cornwall' ('pro quibusdam armaturis inde faciendis ad opus comitis Cornubie'), for which he was paid in Dumfries on 12 August 'by special command of the king himself'.[24] A few days later Gaveston was definitely in Sanquhar, about 25 miles north-west of Dumfries; he held a feast there on 17 August, no doubt to celebrate his elevation to the earldom

---

[18] PRO E 101/373/15, fo. 25[r], under date of 24 Aug.: 'Roberto le Somnour, garcioni domini P. de Gavaston', venienti cum litteris regis de partibus Scocie usque London' et de ibidem revertenti cum litteris thesaurarii et aliorum pro negociis ipsius regis, pro expensis suis redeundo, per manus proprias, iij s.'

[19] This would have given him time to make the journey to Scotland via London and be back London by 24 Aug. The letter which he had brought from Gaveston presumably announced his master's imminent return to England.   [20] Foedera: R. II. i. 2.

[21] Ibid. 49–50.

[22] Hamilton, Gaveston, p. 139 n. 1; PRO E 101/373/15, fo. 21[v]: 'xiij die augusti, Roberto de Rufford', valleto domini P. de Gavaston' leso veniendo de partibus Pontivi in comitiva dicti domini sui et moranti London' pro eadem lesione sananda, de dono regis nomine sustentacionis sue ibidem morando, per manus proprias ibidem [sc. London'], xvj s.'

[23] PRO E 101/373/15, fos. 37[r], 39[v], 51[r].   [24] Ibid., fo. 9[r].

of Cornwall. The feast was attended by the king and also apparently by the earls of Lincoln, Lancaster, and Hereford, all three of whom dined with the king on that day; one of them, Lancaster, even supplied one minstrel for the feast.[25]

The earldom of Cornwall and the charter of 6 August 1307

Whether or not the recall of Gaveston was the first act of Edward of Carnarvon as king, the grant of the earldom of Cornwall to him was without doubt Edward's first royal charter.[26] The document, dated at Dumfries on 6 August in the first year of the king's reign, has survived in the original, although the *Annales Paulini* claim that it was burnt by the earls when Gaveston left for Ireland on his second exile, in the summer of 1308.[27] The substance of the charter does not present any particular difficulty or abnormal characteristic. The reason for its great length is simply that the appurtenances of the earldom of Cornwall and the extent of the other lands which had once belonged to the late earl Edmund and were now transferred to Gaveston were considerable. In many ways, however, the charter is quite exceptional and possibly unique. Its unusual features concern its date, witnesses, handwriting, and decoration, not to mention the peculiarities of its enrolment on the Charter Roll.

As we have already seen, Chancellor Ralph Baldock continued to seal writs of course with Edward I's great seal until 25 July 1307, on which day he obtained confirmation of the old king's death.[28] Four days later, on 29 July, he received a privy seal writ ordering him to send to the new king, then in Carlisle, the great seal of Edward I, which was in his custody, or some other seal. Baldock obeyed and on 2 August two of his own clerks, Richard of Loughborough and John de Munden, and the chancery clerk Hugh de Burgh left London for Carlisle with Edward I's great seal.[29] Clerks could not be expected to travel as fast as express messengers; it probably took them about a week to get to Carlisle, by which time Edward II had moved to Dumfries, a further 30 miles away. Examination of the seal which is

---

[25] Ibid., fo. 19ʳ; Maddicott, *Lancaster*, pp. 71, 75.
[26] PRO E 41/460 (Chaplais, *ERD*, pl. 8*b*); PRO C 53/94, m. 9 (*Foedera*: R. II. i. 2).
[27] *Ann. Paul.*, p. 263; Hamilton, *Gaveston*, pp. 146–7 n. 1.
[28] *Foedera*: R. I. ii. 1018.   [29] Ibid.

still attached to the original charter for Gaveston shows that it is an impression made from the matrix of Edward I's great seal, which had been sent from London to Carlisle, but, before it was used to seal the charter, the matrix had been altered by the addition, on the majesty side, of two castles in the field, apparently in memory of Edward II's mother, Eleanor of Castile; Edward I's great seal had thus become his son's great seal.[30] The alteration to the matrix, probably carried out by a local goldsmith, need not have taken very long, but it was a further source of delay and the charter could not possibly have been sealed as early as 6 August at Dumfries. The sealing could have taken place as late as 17 August, the day of the Gaveston feast at Sanquhar, but no later: next day, 18 August, privy seal writs began to be sent out, ordering John Langton, bishop of Chichester, the new royal chancellor, to issue documents under the great seal.[31] By then the seal was evidently no longer with the king; it was either on its way, or about to be sent, to the chancery somewhere in the south. While the seal had been in the king's custody, it had been used to authenticate four documents only, all connected with the grant of the earldom of Cornwall to Gaveston and all dated 6 August at Dumfries: one was the charter itself and the other three were letters and writs subsidiary to the charter.[32] That the king had wanted the seal for the sole purpose of authenticating these four documents is beyond question. Nor is there any doubt therefore that he had already decided to grant the earldom of Cornwall to Gaveston when, during the week which ended on 29 July, he ordered Baldock to send him Edward I's great seal.[33] On at least one of the two occasions on which, in June 1308, the king was again to 'borrow' the seal, it was for the authentication of other documents connected with Gaveston.[34]

It is probable that, when, on 16 June 1308, Edward II intimated to Clement V and Philip the Fair that, at the time of the grant of the earldom of Cornwall to Gaveston, the latter was unaware of it and absent (that is to say, out of the country),[35] he equated the time of the grant with the official date of the sealed charter, 6 August 1307. But

---

[30] Wyon, pl. VII (nos. 47–8: Edward I), VIII (nos. 49–50: Edward II).
[31] PRO C 81/58/1A (*CPR 1307–1313*, p. 3).
[32] *CChR* iii. 108; *CPR 1307–1313*, p. 9; *CCR 1307–1313*, p. 12.
[33] *Foedera*: R. I. ii. 1018.
[34] Ibid.: R. II. i. 49–51; *CPR 1307–1313*, p. 83; *Parl. Writs*, II. ii, app. pp. 14–15.
[35] *Foedera*: R. II. i. 49–50.

why had the charter been so dated in the first place? In normal circumstances a royal charter of the period would have been written and sealed in chancery, perhaps on receipt of a royal privy seal writ ordering its issue, in which case the place-date and time-date of the charter would most probably have been copied from the writ.[36] The notorious vagaries of the chancery's dating practices, however, might easily have produced a very different result such as dating from the day of receipt of the privy seal warrant, backdating, or some other fictitious dating.[37] In fact, as we have seen, the charter was sealed in Scotland, where the king and his wardrobe were, miles away from the chancery, which had remained in London after Edward I's death. It was also in Scotland that the charter was written; its scribe was not a member of the chancery staff, but a clerk of Edward II's wardrobe, Thomas de Newhay, who identifies himself in an autograph and possibly unique note on the right-hand side of the turn-up of the charter, 'T. de Newehagh' scripsit'.[38] Since the king and his wardrobe were in Dumfries on 6 August, the possibility that on that day the king ordered the charter to be written and that it was actually written on the same day cannot be ruled out.

We may note in passing that 6 August 1307 was a Sunday, but, contrary perhaps to what we might have expected, it was not unusual in the early fourteenth century for a royal charter or any other type of royal document, whatever its seal, great seal or privy seal, to be dated on a Sunday.[39] Even sealing on Sundays was not abnormal in the English royal chancery, at least until 1320.[40] The papal chancery itself was not averse to Sunday dating: for the period 1305–8, there have survived seven original bulls of Clement V connected with England which are dated on a Sunday;[41] indeed one of them bears the same date as the charter for Gaveston, 6 August 1307.[42]

From the pontificate of Calixtus III, 6 August became an important date in the ecclesiastical calendar. After the defeat of the Turks before Belgrade on 6 August 1456, Calixtus decreed that the

[36] Maxwell-Lyte, *Great Seal*, p. 247.

[37] Ibid., pp. 243–54; Chaplais, *ERD*, p. 18.

[38] PRO E 41/460; Chaplais, *ERD*, pl. 8b.

[39] For privy seal writs so dated, see e.g. *Cal. Chanc. War.* i. 266, 267, 269, 270, 271, 272, 274, 275.   [40] Maxwell-Lyte, *Great Seal*, p. 296.

[41] Zutshi, *Original Papal Letters in England, 1305–1415*, nos. 1, 21, 25, 45, 47, 54, 55.

[42] Ibid., no. 47.

event should be commemorated throughout the Christian Church by celebrating on that day, as from 1457, the feast of the 'Transfiguratio Domini'. This was not, however, a true innovation, because there were a few rare churches which had celebrated the Transfiguration on 6 August (instead of the second Sunday in Lent) for a number of years; one of them had done so from the thirteenth century, the Benedictine abbey of St Albans,[43] only about 6 miles away as the crow flies from the manor of King's Langley, Edward II's favourite place of residence;[44] it was also at King's Langley that Gaveston was eventually laid to rest in January 1315.[45] That the charter for Gaveston was dated 6 August deliberately rather than by chance is suggested by the fact that, of all the documents of the reign sealed with the great seal, the charter and associated letters and writs are the earliest, not to be followed by any other until 18 August, the day after the Gaveston feast at Sanquhar.[46] The implication, however sacrilegious it may seem, is obvious. A simple knight, only one of a whole army of 267 young men knighted in May 1306,[47] had been transfigured into an earl, one of the king's *socii*.[48] The earldom to which he succeeded had been that of Edmund, son of Richard, king of the Romans, and grandson of King John. Furthermore it was an earldom which Edward I had intended to bestow, had he lived long enough, on one of his two younger sons.[49] The new king had brushed

---

[43] R. T. Hampson, *Medii Aevi Kalendarium*, ii (London, 1841), 176; *English Benedictine Kalendars after AD 1100*, ed. F. Wormald, i (London, 1939), 31, 33, 41.

[44] Johnstone, *Edw. of Carnarvon*, pp. 28–30, 65; Tout, *Place of Edw. II*, p. 156.

[45] *Vita*, pp. 58–9; Tout, *Place of Edw. II*, p. 156; Conway Davies, *Baron. Opp.*, p. 85; Hamilton, *Gaveston*, pp. 99–100.

[46] *CChR* iii. 107; *CCR 1307–1313*, p. 1; *CPR 1307–1313*, p. 3; *CFR 1307–1319*, pp. 1–3; *Foedera*: R. II. i. 3–4.

[47] W. A. Shaw, *The Knights of England* (London, 1906), i. 112 (where the date for Gaveston's knighting should be corrected from 22 to 26 May 1306); Hamilton, *Gaveston*, p. 32.

[48] 'Comites dicuntur quasi socii regis' (Marcel David, *La Souveraineté et les limites juridiques du pouvoir monarchique du IXe au XVe siècle* (Paris, 1954), p. 250 n. 23; B. Wilkinson, *Studies in the Constitutional History of the Thirteenth and Fourteenth Centuries*, 2nd edn. (Manchester University Press, 1952), pp. 249–50).

[49] *Brit. Chron.*, p. 456; *Vita*, p. 15: 'Dominus Edwardus rex senior uni ex filiis suis Thome uel Edmundo comitatum Cornubie contulisse decreuerat; sed mors amara preueniens factum quod erat conueniens fecit imperfectum'; *Ann. Lond.*, p. 151: 'eidem Petro . . . contulit comitatum Cornubie, duobus fratribus predicti regis non promotis'; *Flores*, iii. 139: 'rex contulit dicto Petro . . . comitatum Cornubie, qui nulli priscis temporibus dari consueverat nisi progenitis ex stirpe regali'. Trokelowe (p. 65) says of the county of Cornwall: 'specialiter spectat ad coronam'; the author of the *Vita* raises the same point (p. 1): 'cum dubitaretur an rex predictum comitatum a jure quod cum corona habebat posset separare', adding that the earl of Lincoln had suggested

aside his father's wishes and preferred his adoptive brother to his two half-brothers Thomas of Brotherton and Edmund of Woodstock. Gaveston had indeed arrived.

It has often been pointed out that the charter for Gaveston is witnessed by seven earls, those of Lincoln, Lancaster, Surrey, Hereford, Arundel, Richmond, and Pembroke, an indication that they all approved of the grant or at least did not object to it.[50] In his letters of 16 June 1308 to Clement V and Philip the Fair, the king claimed that the grant had been made not only with the advice and consent of the earls, but even at their instigation ('ad procuracionem').[51] It is difficult to believe that it was at the suggestion of any of the earls, except perhaps Lincoln, that the grant was made, but there is no reason to disbelieve that they agreed to it.[52] What may be worth adding about the list of witnesses to the charter is that it consists of earls only; the absence of bishops from the list is not unique among the early charters of the reign, but that of officials of the royal household and of anybody below the rank of earl is unusual and perhaps deliberate.[53]

Another unusual feature of the charter is its decoration with pen and ink.[54] Along the borders, the Gaveston eagles alternate with Cornish choughs with red beaks and legs. In the letter 'E' of 'Edwardus', the first word of the charter, above the central horizontal bar, there is a shield with the royal arms, namely the three leopards of

---

that the king could alienate the county as other kings had done twice before. As pointed out by K. B. McFarlane, 'Had Edward I a "Policy" towards the Earls?', *History*, 50 (1965), 157–8, Cornwall came to Edward I, when Earl Edmund died, by inheritance rather than by escheat to the crown. It was also as his father's heir that Edward II acquired it.

[50] Maddicott, *Lancaster*, pp. 70–1; Phillips, *Pembroke*, p. 27 n. 1; Hamilton, *Gaveston*, p. 37; Tout, *Place of Edw. II*, p. 14 and n. 5.

[51] *Foedera*: R. II. i. 49–50.

[52] It was the view of the author of the *Vita* that some magnates advised, and agreed to, the grant (p. 1); later on (p. 15), he says that the barons resented it; see also *Ann. Lond.*, p. 151.

[53] The next two charters, both grants of free warren issued in pursuance of warrants under the privy seal, are dated 21 Aug. at Cumnock and 29 Aug. at Sanquhar respectively (PRO C 53/94, m. 10, nos. 10 and 7 (*CChR* iii. 107): the first is witnessed by the earls of Lincoln, Lancaster, Hereford, and Arundel, Aymer de Valence (not yet earl of Pembroke), Hugh le Despenser, and Robert Clifford; the second is witnessed by the earls of Lincoln, Lancaster, Surrey, and Arundel, Henry de Percy, Hugh le Despenser, Robert Clifford, and Miles Stapelton, steward of the king's household).

[54] See Elizabeth Danbury, 'The Decoration and Illumination of Royal Charters in England, 1250–1509: An Introduction', *England and her Neighbours*, ed. Michael Jones and Malcolm Vale (London, 1989), p. 164 n. 28.

England; below the bar, there is another shield made up of two half-shields placed side by side, but not properly dimidiated; in the left half, three eagles displayed (looking left), arranged along a vertical line, are meant to represent one half of the Gaveston arms; in the right half, three complete chevrons, i.e. the arms of the Clare family. In the centre of the upper margin of the charter, there is a large eagle displayed. Over the eagle three shields are drawn: in the centre, that is to say over the main body of the eagle, the royal shield with the three leopards of England; on the left, over one wing of the eagle, a shield with five eagles displayed (looking right); on the right, over the other wing, the Clare shield with three chevrons. There is no doubt that the shield with five eagles is meant to be the Gaveston shield, but it should have six eagles, not five, as we learn from the Great Parliamentary Roll of Arms of c. 1312: 'Le Counte de Cornewaille de vert a vj Egles de or'.[55] It looks as if the person responsible for the decoration of the charter was not particularly competent in heraldic matters. Another puzzling point is the inclusion of the arms of the Clare family. Since Gaveston did not marry Margaret de Clare, sister of the young earl of Gloucester, until 1 November 1307,[56] the Clare arms should not appear on a charter dated on the previous 6 August. Two possible explanations come to mind: either the charter was decorated later than 1 November; or the marriage had already been arranged (perhaps in the form of a betrothal or 'sponsalia per verba de futuro') well before 6 August, and the Clare arms were associated with Gaveston's arms on the charter in anticipation of the forth-coming marriage ('matrimonium per verba de presenti'). The mistake regarding the number of eagles on Gaveston's shield suggests that the artist, whoever he was, did not belong to the Gaveston household. Perhaps he was the scribe of the charter, Thomas de Newhay, a clerk of the king's household. He was at any rate someone familiar with the order of precedence traditionally followed in original documents, for

[55] A. R. Wagner, *A Catalogue of English Mediaeval Rolls of Arms* (Soc. of Antiquaries, London, 1950), p. 42. The pressmark on the leather case in which Gaveston's charters of 1309 to the king were stored in the treasury consisted of one large eagle displayed (Palgrave, *Antient Kalendars*, i. 51). Also inside the letter 'E,' on the left of the shields, there is a drawing of an animal, apparently a bat with one head and two bodies. See Plate I.

[56] Guisborough, p. 380 n. *a*; *Vita*, p. 2; *Ann. Paul.*, p. 258; Hamilton, *Gaveston*, p. 38; below, nn. 64–5. Margaret's shield, after her marriage, represented the Gaveston arms dimidiating Clare; see G. E. Cokayne, *Complete Peerage*, iii (London, 1913), p. 433 n. *d*.

example in the subscriptions attached to solemn papal privileges: the place of honour is for the king's shield, uppermost or in the centre; the other two shields are in a respectful position, either below or beside the royal arms, the six eagles of Gaveston, earl of Cornwall, on the left, having precedence over the three Clare chevrons, on the right.[57] The large Gaveston eagle with its wings spread out, in the centre of the upper margin, seems to be watching over the combined destinies of the royal house and of the houses of Gaveston and Clare. The inclusion of Cornish choughs in the decoration needs no explanation.

Copies of the Gaveston charter and of the three writs subsidiary to it were in due course (perhaps as late as December 1307) delivered into the chancery for enrolment on the appropriate rolls: the charter is enrolled on the Charter Roll of the first year of the king's reign, on a separate membrane, and the writs patent and close respectively on the Patent Roll of the same year between entries dated 16 and 18 October, and on the Close Roll, also of the first year, below an entry dated 10 December and above another of 25 November.[58] In the meantime the grant had been confirmed in the Michaelmas parliament at Northampton.[59]

There is ample evidence that adoptive brothers everywhere regarded one another as blood-brothers. In pagan societies, the adoption ceremony sometimes included a ritual in which each of the two prospective brothers opened a vein and gave his partner some of his blood to drink, or a mixture of the two bloods was drunk by both; thus they could truly say that they were 'brothers of one blood'.[60] The same ritual is known to have been occasionally observed by Christians, although it seems to have been more usual for them to take part in a communion service in which the two partners shared the same host.[61] Whatever ceremony, if any, had taken place when Edward of Carnarvon and Gaveston made their compact of adoptive brotherhood, there is no doubt that Edward as king treated Gaveston

---

[57] On papal solemn privileges, the pope's subscription is placed uppermost and in the centre; below it, the subscriptions of the cardinal bishops form the middle column; those of the cardinal priests are in the left column, and those of the cardinal deacons are in the right column; in the rota, the name 'Sanctus Petrus' is on the left and 'Sanctus Paulus' on the right; see e.g. Albert Brackmann, *Papsturkunden* (Leipzig, 1914), pl. VII, a solemn privilege of Innocent II.

[58] PRO C 53/94, m. 9 (*CChR* iii. 108); PRO C 54/125, m. 14 (*CCR 1307–1313*, p. 12); PRO C 66/129, m. 17 (*CPR 1307–1313*, p. 9). [59] *Lanercost*, p. 210.

[60] Keen, 'Brotherhood in Arms', p. 4. [61] Ibid., pp. 3–4.

as his blood-brother, giving him precedence over his two half-brothers
Thomas and Edmund, both (or at least one) of whom may in any case
not even have been born at the time the compact was made.[62] Nobody
else in England, however, regarded the Gascon as any kind of brother
to the king, and it was one of the objections to his creation as earl of
Cornwall that he did not belong to the royal line.[63] For this there was
no remedy; the only step which the king could and did take was to
bring Gaveston into the royal family circle through the back door, by
giving him in marriage his niece Margaret de Clare, daughter of his
late sister Joan and of her first husband Gilbert, earl of Gloucester.
The marriage took place on All Saints' Day 1307 at Berkhamsted.[64]
It was attended by the king, who added a personal touch to the
proceedings by providing £7. 10s. 6d. in pennies, which were thrown
over the heads of the bride and groom, at the door of the church, as
they were about to enter.[65]

Gaveston as regent; the first ever great seal of absence and its origins

Three months after Gaveston's wedding, Edward II left for France, in
January 1308, for the celebration of his own marriage to Isabella,
daughter of Philip the Fair.[66] Before departing, he had had to appoint
someone who would rule the kingdom in his name during his absence.
On such occasions in the past, the duties of regent had normally fallen

[62] Thomas of Brotherton was born on 1 June 1300 and Edmund of Woodstock on 5 Aug.
1301 (*Brit. Chron.*, pp. 38–9).

[63] *Vita*, p. 16: 'Publice tamen scitur quod non erat filius regis nec regalem prosapiam
quicquid attingens'; Maddicott, *Lancaster*, p. 71.

[64] Guisborough, p. 380 n. *a*; *Vita*, p. 2; *Ann. Paul.*, p. 258; Hamilton, *Gaveston*, p. 38. In
Trokelowe (p. 67), the marriage is wrongly placed after Gaveston's Irish exile.

[65] Hamilton, *Gaveston*, p. 38; PRO E 101/373/15, fo. 22ʳ: 'Primo die novembris, videlicet in
festo Omnium Sanctorum, in denariis liberatis ipsi regi apud Berkhamstede ad nupcias domini
P. de Gavaston' et filie comitis Glouc' videlicet projectis ibidem ad hostium ecclesie ultra capita
dictorum domini Petri et uxoris sue eodem die in introitu eorumdem in ecclesia predicta, per
manus Willelmi de Boudon' liberantis denarios eidem regi apud Berkhamstede, vij li. x s. vj d.';
it is likely that in this instance the words *denariis* and *denarios* are used in the literal sense of
'pennies'.

[66] For recent discussions of various aspects of the marriage, see Elizabeth A. R. Brown, 'The
Political Repercussions of Family Ties in the Early Fourteenth Century: The Marriage of
Edward II of England and Isabelle of France', *Speculum*, 63 (1988), 573–95; 64 (1989), 373–9;
ead., *Customary Aids and Royal Finance in Capetian France* (Medieval Academy Books, no. 100,
Cambridge, Mass., 1992), pp. 11–33.

on the justiciar or on a close member of the royal family. Under Henry III it had been the justiciar until the justiciarship was abolished in the latter part of the reign. When there was no justiciar, Henry appointed members of his family, for example Queen Eleanor of Provence and his brother Richard, earl of Cornwall, in 1253–4 (the latter acting on his own in the last seven months), and again Richard in January–February 1264. In the next reign, apart from the exceptional period which ran from the death of Henry III to the return of Edward I from the Crusade, it was also a member of the royal family who ruled the kingdom when the king was abroad. Edmund, earl of Cornwall, acted as regent during Edward I's long absence in France from 1286 to 1289, as his father Richard had done twice under Henry III. While the king was in Flanders in 1297–8, the regent was Edward of Carnarvon, only a boy of 13 at the time.[67]

In January 1308 Edward II might have given the regency to either of his two half-brothers Thomas and Edmund. It is true that they were only 7 and 6 years old respectively at the time, but considerations of age did not deter Edward III from appointing as regents his first son Edward when he was only 8 in 1338, his second son Lionel when he was 6 in 1345, and his youngest son Thomas before he had even reached his first birthday in 1355.[68] As in the matter of the earldom of Cornwall, however, the two half-brothers were passed over to make room for Piers Gaveston, the adoptive brother and nephew-in-law. It cannot be argued as an excuse that Gaveston's two predecessors as earls of Cornwall had in their lifetime held the post of regent, because each of them had been related to the reigning king by blood whereas Gaveston was not, but it should be remembered that in Edward II's eyes adoptive brotherhood was as good as blood relationship. Whatever claims may have been made to support Gaveston's appointment, the contemporaries were not impressed. '*Mira res*,' wrote the author of the *Vita*, 'yesterday's exile and outcast has been made governor and keeper of the land.'[69] Gaveston was appointed *custos regni* and royal lieutenant on 26 December 1307 and his powers were set out in letters patent dated at Dover on 18 January 1308.[70] The king must have known that he would be out of England for a

---

[67] For an excellent survey of the regency problems, see *Brit. Chron.*, pp. 31–2, 38.
[68] Ibid., pp. 39–40.   [69] *Vita*, p. 3.   [70] *Foedera*: R. II. i. 24, 28.

short while only; in fact he sailed from Dover on 22 January at dawn and was back there at 3 o'clock in the afternoon of 7 February.[71] Yet the measures he took for the government of the realm while he was away were unprecedented. Never in the two previous reigns had such wide powers been conferred on a regent. In the matter of ecclesiastical elections, for example, earlier regents had not been allowed to grant a *congé d'élire* or to assent to an election if the value of the church concerned exceeded 50 marks a year; in such cases the king himself had had to be sued abroad, wherever he was.[72] No such restrictions were imposed on Gaveston: his powers applied to all churches, cathedral as well as conventual, regardless of their wealth, which were in need of a new pastor.[73] He could also receive oaths of fealty from those elected, order temporalities to be restored to them, present to benefices which were in the king's gift, and deal with wardships and marriages.[74] The clerical work involved in these matters was unlikely to cause any particular difficulty for the regent, because the chancery was to remain in England. Only in their attestation would the required letters and writs patent and close differ from those issued while the king was in England: their protocol would begin 'Edwardus' etc. as usual, but they would be attested by the regent ('Teste P. de Gavaston', comite Cornubie')[75] instead of the normal attestation by the king himself ('Teste me ipso'); the routine writs of course to be issued by the chancery while the king was away would be similarly attested by the regent. Only one outstanding problem had to be attended to: because the great seal, without which the chancery could not function, was to go abroad with the king, a duplicate or a substitute for it had to be provided for the regent's use in England.

[71] Ibid. 29, 31; *Gascon Rolls*, iv, ed. Y. Renouard, p. xiii.

[72] Susan Wood, *English Monasteries and their Patrons in the Thirteenth Century* (Oxford University Press, 1955), p. 70 and nn.; Maxwell-Lyte, *Great Seal*, p. 170; *The Charters of Norwich Cathedral Priory*, i, ed. Barbara Dodwell (Pipe Roll Society, NS xl, 1974), no. 55.

[73] *Foedera*: R. II. i. 28.   [74] Ibid.

[75] For an example of a chancery document issued in England under the regent's attestation in 1287, while Edward I was in France, see Chaplais, *ERD*, pl. 6; see also ibid., pp. 16, 49. More details on the regency system will be found in Maxwell-Lyte, *Great Seal*, pp. 168–78. When the reduplication procedure followed for the great seal was extended to the privy seal under Henry V, no such distinction was made between privy seal documents issued in England in the king's absence and those issued by the king in France (Chaplais, *EMDP* I. ii, no. 395); this was due to the absence of an attestation clause in privy seal documents in general. Examples of chancery documents issued in England while Gaveston was regent in 1308 will be found in *Foedera*: R. II. i. 30; *Parl. Writs*, II. ii, app. p. 9; *CPR 1307–1313*, pp. 44–5.

On a number of occasions Edward II's father and grandfather had experienced the need for the concurrent use of two great seals or at least of two seals of authority equal to that of the great seal, one at home and the other abroad. There was a long tradition in England, going back at least as far as the reign of Henry II, for the simultaneous use at home of two great seals, which at the time of composition of the *Dialogus de Scaccario* (in the late 1170s) were identical in size, design, legend, and authority, one for the itinerant chancery and the other for the stationary exchequer at Westminster.[76] Although by Henry III's reign the exchequer seal was smaller than the chancery great seal and differed from it in several other respects, both still had the same authority.[77] For this reason, during each of Henry's first four visits to France, the exchequer seal was used by the chancery in England instead of the great seal, namely in 1230, 1242–3, 1253–4, and 1259–60: on the first, second, and fourth occasions, the great seal went to France with the king ('First Great Seal' on the first and second occasions; 'Second Great Seal' on the fourth);[78] exceptionally, in 1253–4, it remained in England sealed up in a pouch, and the king took abroad with him a small seal which had been especially engraved for his use in Gascony.[79] The exchequer seal, however, was not a satisfactory substitute for the great seal, because it was needed in its own department, and alternative arrangements had to be made for the sealing of exchequer writs. In 1259–60, as a replacement for its seal on loan to the chancery, the exchequer was given a substitute,

[76] *Dialogus de Scaccario*, ed. C. Johnson (Nelson's Medieval Classics, 1950), p. 62; Chaplais, *ERD*, p. 46. For a third exchequer writ of Henry II not mentioned in *ERD*, see *The Beauchamp Cartulary, 1100–1268*, ed. Emma Mason (Pipe Roll Society, NS xliii, 1980), no. 173 (a writ of naifty).

[77] In Henry III's reign, however, at least in 1242–3 and in 1262, the exchequer seal looked more like a privy seal than a great seal; see Chaplais, *ERD*, pl. 4a, and nn. For examples of exchequer seals from Edward I onwards, see H. Jenkinson, 'The Great Seal of England: Deputed or Departmental Seals', *Archaeologia*, 85 (1936), 297–8 and pl. LXXXIV.

[78] See Tout, *Chapters*, i. 207, 291–2, 303 (in need of revision); Maxwell-Lyte, *Great Seal*, p. 315. What is called here the 'First Great Seal' is the normal great seal used from the beginning of Henry III's reign until the treaty of Paris of 1259 (Wyon, 'First Seal', pl. VI, nos. 41–2; Birch, 'First Seal'); the legend on the obverse reads: HENRICVS DEI GRATIA REX ANGLIE DOMINVS HYBERNIE, and on the reverse: HENRICVS DVX NORMANNIE ET AQUITANIE COMES ANDEGAVIE. The 'Second Great Seal' is the normal great seal used from the treaty of Paris to the end of the reign (Wyon, 'Second Seal', pl. VII, nos. 43–4; Birch, 'Third Seal', no. 119; see Chaplais, *EMDA* I. 235–53); the legend on the obverse and on the reverse, with occasional variants in the lettering, e.g. 'DVX' and 'DUX', reads: HEꞐRICUS DEI GRACIA REX AꞐGLIE DOMꞐVS HYBERꞐIE DVX AQVITAꞐꞐIE.

[79] Tout, *Chapters*, i. 292–3; the small seal used in Gascony is reproduced in *Archaeologia*, 85, pl. LXXXIX, nos. 1–2.

about which we only know that until then it had been kept by Edward of Westminster under the seal of Henry Wingham, bishop elect of London,[80] chancellor. This was apparently the last time that the exchequer seal was used in chancery as a substitute for the great seal. By 1262 a special seal ('Substitute Great Seal') had been engraved for that purpose.[81] It was used for the government of the realm while Henry III was in France with the normal great seal of the period (Second Great Seal) from July to December of that year.[82] When Henry again visited France in September–October 1263 and in January–February 1264, the opposite solution was adopted: the Second Great Seal remained in England and the Substitute Great Seal went to France with the king, who used it there and continued to use it for a time after his return to England, because the normal great seal (Second Great Seal), it seems, was then in baronial hands.[83] Smaller than the First Great Seal and Second Great Seal by about one-sixth, the Substitute Great Seal differs from both in its design, resembling the First Great Seal in some of its features (notably in the representation of the royal throne on the obverse), while being closer to the Second Great Seal in others (for example, in the emblems held in the king's hands, also on the obverse). The legend on the obverse reproduces the wording of the First Great Seal ([H]EℵRICUS DE[I GRACIA RE]X AℵGLIE [DOMIℵUS HY]BERℵIE), whereas the reverse has exactly the same legend as the reverse of the Second Great Seal ([HEℵRICUS DEI GRACIA R]EX AℵGLIE [DOMIℵUS HYBERℵI]E DUX AQVITAℵℵI[E]).[84] Another interesting point is that the Substitute

---

[80] Tout, *Chapters*, vi. 118; *Close Rolls 1259–1261*, pp. 12–13.

[81] The 'Substitute Great Seal' is the seal described in Wyon (p. 23) as the 'Third Seal'; the seal reproduced there on pl. VII, nos. 45–6, however, is not the 'Substitute Great Seal', but the 'Substitute Great Seal Prototype' (see below), which has a different legend.

[82] Tout, *Chapters*, i. 304 n. 1; *CLR 1260–1267*, p. 112; *CPR 1258–1266*, pp. 224, 226, 228; Maxwell-Lyte, *Great Seal*, p. 60.

[83] *Foedera*: R. I. ii. 433; Tout, *Chapters*, i. 305–6; *CChR* ii. 183. The letters patent and charters sealed with the 'Substitute Great Seal' in Jan.–Feb. 1264 in France and in Feb.–Mar. 1264 in England after Henry's return are enrolled on a separate roll (*CPR 1258–1266*, pp. 376–84; for the enrolment of those sealed in England with the 'Second Great Seal', see ibid., pp. 305–6).

[84] Two impressions of the 'Substitute Great Seal' have been noticed: one, very fragmentary, is in Paris, Archives Nationales, J 630, no. 19 (L. Douët d'Arcq, *Collection de sceaux* (Paris, 1863), iii, no. 10013; Amiens, 23 Jan. 1264; *CPR 1258–1266*, p. 378); the other, slightly damaged, is in Canterbury Cathedral Archives, Charta antiqua C. 78 (a charter dated at Rochester, 27 Feb. 1264; *CPR 1258–1266*, p. 383). See Plate III. For the obverse, the end of the legend, missing on the Canterbury seal, has been supplied from Douët d'Arcq, no. 10013.

Great Seal is an exact replica of an earlier seal ('Substitute Great Seal Prototype'), except that the legend on the reverse of the prototype is the same as in the First Great Seal instead of the Second Great Seal, presumably because its matrix was made before the treaty of Paris of 1259.[85] Whether the Substitute Great Seal is in fact the Substitute Great Seal Prototype with an altered legend is uncertain, because on the obverse, which has the same legend on the two seals and therefore required no alteration, the shape of some of the letters N and V is not the same in both. The prototype may have been the seal kept by Edward of Westminster under Wingham's seal and used in 1259–60 as a substitute for the exchequer seal.[86]

In Edward I's reign a small seal was also used as a substitute for the great seal when the king went abroad. Edward took it with him to France in 1279, the normal great seal remaining in England.[87] It was probably the same substitute, also a small seal, which the regent used for the government of England while the king was in Gascony with the great seal from 1286 to 1289 and in Flanders, also with the great seal, in 1297–8; in the latter case the regent was Edward of Carnarvon.[88] Whether the substitute for the great seal in Edward I's reign was modelled on its predecessor of the 1260s cannot, unfortunately, be established, because no extant impression has so far been traced.

The foregoing evidence shows that by 1308 the institution of substitutes for the great seal had been in existence for almost fifty years. Edward II himself had had first-hand experience of it when, in his father's reign, he acted as regent in 1297–8. The matrix of the great seal substitute which he had used then could have been adapted for Gaveston's regency, in the same way as he had adapted his late

[85] This prototype is known only from a cast (BL Seals li. 18 and 19; Birch, 'Second Seal', no. 118). The lost original seal, which was already damaged when the cast was made, was apparently used, after it had been further damaged, for Wyon, pl. vii, nos. 45–6. The legend reads on the obverse: HEηRICVS DEI GRACIA REX AηGLIE DOMIηUS HYBERηIE, and on the reverse: HENRICVS DVX NORMANNIE ET AQUI[TANNIE COMES ANDE]GAVIE. On the reverse, the point of the king's sword touches the last letter of the word [ANDE]GAVIE, as in Wyon, pl. vii, no. 46 ([ANDEGAV]IE), whereas in the 'Substitute Great Seal' it touches the second minim of the first η of AQVITAηηI[E]. See Plate II.

[86] Tout, *Chapters*, vi. 118; *Close Rolls 1259–1261*, pp. 12–13.

[87] Maxwell-Lyte, *Great Seal*, pp. 315–16 (where the seal is incorrectly described as Edward I's privy seal); *Rôles gascons*, ii, ed. C. Bémont, nos. 267, 284, 286, 302, 306, 313, 316–19, etc.

[88] Maxwell-Lyte, *Great Seal*, p. 316; Tout, *Chapters*, ii. 12, 68; PRO E 159/70, m. 35d. The matrix of the seal was not broken up until 4 June 1320, shortly before Edward II left for France (*Foedera*: R. II. i. 428; *CCR 1318–1323*, pp. 237–8).

father's normal great seal for the use of his own chancery early in August 1307, by adding on the obverse two castles in the field.[89] But shortly before sailing for France, Edward decided to have a new substitute engraved instead. The work was done by the London goldsmith Simon de Keyles between 14 and 21 January 1308: on the first of these dates Keyles received from the wardrobe a prest of £5 for his forthcoming work on the seal, and on the second the king handed over in person the seal to the chancellor 'for the government of the realm whilst the king should happen to be staying outside the same realm' (*pro regimine regni dum extra idem regnum dictum regem morari contigerit*).[90] Unlike the great seal substitutes of the two previous reigns, which were either taken abroad by the king or left in England for the regent's use, the new seal was intended to be used, for the first time in English history, specifically as a seal of absence only. After serving as chancery seal while Gaveston was regent from 22 January to 7 February 1308, it was brought into use again twelve years later during the regency of the earl of Pembroke (19 June–22 July 1320).[91] Ironically, the only impression of the seal which has been noticed is attached to a document which falls just outside the second of these regency periods: dated at Sturry (Kent) on 16 June (1320), it is attested by the king himself, not by Pembroke.[92] This was the result of an unforeseen delay in the king's crossing to France, due to the late arrival of his French safe-conduct: as the normal great seal had already been sealed up in a pouch and put away in a safe place, it was

[89] The normal great seal of Edward II is reproduced in Wyon, pl. VIII, nos. 49–50, to be compared with the normal great seal of Edward I (Wyon, pl. VII, nos. 47–8).

[90] Chaplais, *EMDP* I. i. 69; PRO E 403/141, m. 9; E 101/325/4, m. 2; E 101/373/15, fo. 47ʳ; *Foedera*: R. II. i. 29; see also 31.

[91] *Foedera*: R. II. i. 428.

[92] Oxford, Oriel College Archives, DL 9/A. 10; the seal is reproduced on Plate IV. See *Oriel College Records*, ed. C. L. Shadwell and H. E. Salter (Oxford Historical Society, lxxxv, 1926), p. 82, no. 67 and pl. 1 (facing p. 494); Chaplais, *EMDP* I. i. 69; Maxwell-Lyte, *Great Seal*, p. 316. On 14 May 1313 arrangements had also been made for the same seal of absence to be used in England, should Edward take his great seal to France (T. Madox, *The History and Antiquities of the Exchequer* . . ., 2nd edn., i (London, 1769), 75), but in fact, when the king sailed from Dover on 23 May, he only took his privy seal with him, although the two chancery clerks Robert de Askeby and Master Henry de Cliff accompanied him abroad (Maxwell-Lyte, *Great Seal*, p. 52; *Gascon Rolls*, iv, ed. Renouard, p. xvi, and nos. 981–1076, 1503). In some cases, the privy seal was used instead of the great seal (ibid., nos. 981–1076). In others, it was used to seal warrants for the great seal, which were sent to the chancery in England; in such cases, the great seal documents issued in England had the same date and French place of issue as the warrants, and were noted as having been warranted *per breve de privato sigillo* (ibid., nos. 962–3, 968–71, 973–80).

decided that the seal of absence would be used by the king until he sailed and by the regent thereafter.[93]

Like the great seal substitutes of the two previous reigns, Edward II's seal of absence is substantially smaller than his normal great seal and differs from it in details of design on the obverse and reverse. Apart from the inevitable change in the king's name, the legend on both sides of the seal of absence is identical with that of the great seal substitute of the 1260s. On both seals the royal style in the legend of the obverse differs from that of the reverse: on the majesty side the king is simply described as 'by the grace of God king of England, lord of Ireland' and on the equestrian side he is 'by the grace of God king of England, lord of Ireland, duke of Aquitaine', whereas the second of these two styles had invariably been adopted for both sides of the normal great seal ever since the treaty of Paris of 1259. Such similarities and differences need not be attributed to political motives; subservience to tradition is a more likely explanation.

Gaveston's regency passed off uneventfully, although it might well have been otherwise, had he exploited his vice-regal powers to the full instead of acting with such commendable restraint as he seems to have done.[94] It was during his term of office as regent that one of the most disputed ecclesiastical elections of the reign took place. The convent of Westminster, whose abbot, Walter de Wenlok, had died on 25 December 1307, had on the following 10 January obtained a royal licence to elect a new abbot, but by the time the election was made, 26 January 1308, Edward II was in France.[95] It seems incredible that the abbot elect, Richard de Kedyngton, and his supporters might have waited until the king's return, the date of which they could not have guessed, to notify the government of the election. As it turned out, Edward was back in England on 7 February, a long enough delay, but it could have been much longer. What they must have known was that Gaveston had been invested with full power to assent in the king's name to all ecclesiastical elections. If it is true, as Kedyngton's opponents later claimed, that Gaveston had been bribed to engineer the confirmation of the election, what better time could there have been to approach him than during the regency? If it is also

[93] *Foedera*: R. II. i. 428; Chaplais, *EMDA* iv. 152–3.
[94] Hamilton, *Gaveston*, p. 46.
[95] Pearce, *The Monks of Westminster*, pp. 61, 73; *CPR 1307–1313*, p. 34.

true, as again the anti-Kedyngton party alleged some months later, that, when, on 23 February, the king finally gave his assent (significantly perhaps, two days before his coronation at Westminster), it was the third time that he had been sued for it, having declined to grant it on two earlier occasions, could all this have happened within such a short period as sixteen days, from 7 to 23 February?[96] It seems more reasonable to assume that Gaveston was indeed approached for royal assent when he was regent, and that he either refused or, perhaps more probably, told Kedyngton that it would be best to wait until the king returned. What is certain is that he did not confirm the election, although the powers he had been given entitled him to do so. If efforts were made to bribe him on behalf of the abbot elect, they did not succeed, at least while the king was away. By appointing Gaveston as regent, the king had made a grave political error, because this had aroused the jealousy of the other earls. Gaveston's only mistake had been to accept the appointment.

The coronation

The prime responsibility for what happened at the coronation (Sunday, 25 February 1308) must surely also rest on the king's shoulders, since one cannot imagine that even someone as vain and arrogant as Gaveston is unanimously reputed to have been would have taken upon himself to carry the crown of St Edward and walk just in front of the king in the procession.[97] Long before the event, Edward had made up his mind to show the participants in the coronation ceremony how unique his relationship with Gaveston really was: on 26 October 1307 two London upholsterers, John Engayne and John le Tapyter, had received from the wardrobe a prest ∩f £5 'for making tapestries with the arms of the king [or of England]

---

[96] For the king's assent to Kedyngton's election, see ibid., p. 45. On 12 Jan. 1308 a gold ring of the late Wenlok was sent to the king's court at Wye by John de Foxle: 'Anulus auri qui fuit fratris Walteri nuper abbatis Westm' missus ad curiam usque Wy per dominum J. de Foxle xij° die januarii, anno ij° [*sic in MS for* j°]' (Bodl. Lib. MS Tanner 197, fo. 62ʳ). On John de Foxle, see Harvey, *Wenlok*, p. 25. The licence to elect is dated at Wye, 10 Jan. (*CPR 1307–1313*, p. 34).

[97] *Foedera*: R. II. i. 36. The crown was carried by William de Mandeville, earl of Essex and count of Aumale, at Richard I's first coronation in 1189 (Lionel Landon, *The Itinerary of King Richard I* (Pipe Roll Society, NS xiii, 1935), p. 4), and by Richard fitz Alan, earl of Arundel, at Richard II's coronation in 1377 (*Foedera*: R. IV. 9).

and of Piers Gaveston, earl of Cornwall, against the king's coronation'.[98] We do not know, of course, how the arms of the king and those of Gaveston were respectively placed on the tapestries, whether they were side by side or arranged in a way which denoted or at least implied a difference in status, but the mere fact that they appeared together adds significance to some of the puzzling details in the decoration of the charter of 6 August 1307, which has been discussed earlier.

Besides carrying the crown of St Edward, Gaveston performed two other functions at the coronation ceremony: he redeemed *post oblacionem regis* the Curtana sword (or sword of St Edward), which had been carried in the procession by the earl of Lancaster; he also fastened the spur on the king's left foot.[99] So far as we know, none of these functions could be claimed by Gaveston as appertaining to his dignity as earl of Cornwall. If a symbolic significance was attached to the personality of whoever redeemed the Curtana sword or sword of mercy, one might have expected the successor to the now defunct office of justiciar to perform it; Gaveston's function may simply have been to return the sword to safe keeping. It was presumably in his capacity as the king's adoptive brother and according to the king's express wishes that Gaveston carried the crown and walked just in front of him.[100] The same may be true of the fastening of the spur on the king's left foot: in the order of precedence, this placed Edward's adoptive brother immediately after Philip IV's blood-brother, Charles de Valois, who fastened the other spur on the king's right foot.[101]

---

[98] PRO E 101/325/4, m. 2: 'super factura tapetarum de armis regis et domini Petri de Gavaston', comitis Cornubie, contra coronacionem regis'; E 101/373/15, fo. 51^r: 'super factura tapetarum de armis Anglie et domini P. de Gavaston', comitis Cornubie, contra coronacionem regis'; Hamilton, *Gaveston*, p. 145 n. 90. It is possible, of course, although unlikely, that the arms of the king were on one tapestry and those of Gaveston on another.

[99] *Foedera*: R. II. i. 36.   [100] Ibid.   [101] Ibid.

3

EXILE IN IRELAND AND
REHABILITATION

GAVESTON'S undue prominence at the coronation aroused almost universal fury among the English nobility. 'Now for the first time', wrote the author of the *Vita*, 'nearly all the earls and barons of England rose against Piers Gaveston.'[1] This was a reference to the proceedings of the Lent parliament, which met at Westminster on 27 February 1308, two days after the coronation. What happened in that parliament and its continuation at Easter is well known, how the so-called 'three articles' accused Gaveston of treason for accroaching royal power and making himself the king's equal, and how this eventually led to the reversion to the crown of all the vast estates he held as earl of Cornwall, and to his exile, both of which measures were reluctantly sanctioned by the king on 18 May.[2] On that day, royal letters patent in French, issued at Westminster under the great seal, declared that 'mons' Pieres de Gavaston' ', who on this occasion was neither described as earl of Cornwall nor given (understandably in the circumstances) the customary epithets of 'nostre cher et feal', would 'void the kingdom' on the day after the feast of the Nativity of St John the Baptist, and that he, Edward, would do nothing meanwhile to delay or impede his departure.[3] Whoever drafted the document, it certainly was not the king, in whose eyes, as he was to make quite plain in the weeks to come, Gaveston was still earl of Cornwall, although he had temporarily lost the lands which went with the title.

---

[1] *Vita*, p. 4.
[2] Richardson and Sayles, *The Governance of Mediaeval England*, p. 468; *Bridlington*, p. 34; Maddicott, *Lancaster*, pp. 81–2.
[3] *Foedera*: R. II. i. 44; Maddicott, *Lancaster*, pp. 87–8.

For the opposition, however, which included not only most of the earls, but also Archbishop Winchelsey of Canterbury, Gaveston had lost both the earldom and the county of Cornwall. On 24 May the archbishop issued a mandate threatening Gaveston with major excommunication *ipso facto*, if he failed to leave the kingdom by 25 June or presumed to return at any time after that date; with the exception of the king and queen, anyone impeding his departure or abetting his return would incur the same penalty. Winchelsey's mandate referred to Gaveston simply as 'dominus Petrus de Gavaston' ',[4] the exact equivalent in Latin of the French formula used in the letters patent of 18 May.

The title of earl of Cornwall in royal documents: great seal versus privy seal

Between 18 May and the beginning of July, a number of documents were issued in the king's name either for Gaveston himself or for others at his request; some were sealed with the great seal and others with the privy seal, the latter group consisting mainly of warrants ordering the chancellor to issue some of the great seal documents in the first group. Now, as before, the king appeared to control through his privy seal some of the work done in chancery under the great seal, but the surviving evidence shows beyond doubt that this control did not extend to the wording of references to Gaveston. By a privy seal writ dated 10 June at King's Langley, for example, the chancellor was instructed to send a great seal writ of *liberate* to the treasurer and chamberlains of the exchequer, ordering them to pay £1.180 to Gaveston towards his expenses ('quod liberent de thesauro nostro dilecto et fideli nostro Petro de Gavaston', comiti Cornubie').[5] A great seal writ of *liberate* ensued, which omitted the title of earl of Cornwall ('Liberate de thesauro nostro dilecto et fideli nostro Petro de Gavaston' ').[6] Another privy seal warrant, dated 18 June at Newbury, informed the chancellor that the king had granted to his clerk Roger de Clotherum the custody of the smaller piece of the seal for recognizances in the city of York 'a la requeste nostre cher et feal

---

[4] *Reg. Simonis de Gandavo*, i. 237–40. [5] PRO C 81/60/249.
[6] PRO C 62/84, m. 2.

mons' Pierres de Gavaston', counte de Cornwaille' and ordered the issue of great seal letters patent to that effect.[7] The letters patent which were accordingly issued by the chancery stated that the grant had been made 'ad requisicionem dilecti et fidelis nostri Petri de Gavaston' '; once again the title of earl of Cornwall had been omitted.[8] Similarly, in a privy seal writ dated 25 June from Bristol, the king ordered the chancellor to issue great seal protections with the clause 'volumus', valid for one year, 'pro . . . Petro de Gavaston', comite Cornubie', and for others, whereas, in the brief note which on the Patent Roll gives the names of those for whom protections were issued in pursuance of the warrant, the list begins: 'Petrus de Gavaston' ' without the comital title.[9] Other examples of the same kind could be cited, one concerning a pardon for Ralph de Kerres, another relating to the grant of a marriage to Ives de Sulton, etc.[10] Indeed not one single example has been found in which the same discrepancy did not occur between the initiating warrant under the privy seal and the resulting letters under the great seal, although, in every case which has been examined, the great seal letters repeated in their dating-clause the date and place of issue of the privy seal warrant. In some instances in which the warrant indicated that Gaveston had intervened to obtain redress for people who clearly had suffered an injustice, the reference to Gaveston's request was omitted altogether by the chancery, perhaps because it was thought unnecessary, but more plausibly because it reflected on the beneficial aspect of Gaveston's influence at court instead of stressing an improper interference with royal patronage. This happened in the case of *liberate* writs for the repayment of Edward I's debts to two Gascons, Elie Scarlet and his nephew Amauvin Paon of Saint-Emilion.[11] For such editing of the text of royal warrants the chancellor, John Langton, bishop of Chichester, was nominally responsible, but it is evident that neither he nor any of the chancery clerks under him would have gone out of their way so systematically to incur the king's probable displeasure without the specific instructions of the king's council in

---

[7] PRO C 81/60/210.   [8] PRO C 66/130, m. 4 (*CPR 1307–1313*, p. 79).
[9] PRO C 81/60/222; C 66/130, m. 4 (*CPR 1307–1313*, p. 80).
[10] PRO C 81/60/215 and C 66/130, m. 4 (*CPR 1307–1313*, p. 80); PRO C 81/60/246 and C 66/130, m. 3 (*CPR 1307–1313*, p. 83).
[11] PRO C 81/60/258; C 62/84, m. 1 (Woodstock, 5 July 1308).

London and of its most prominent member at the time, the earl of Lincoln, who by then, according to the *Vita*, had become Gaveston's greatest enemy ('maximus inimicus et persecutor').[12]

Various charters and letters patent under the great seal were issued for Gaveston alone or for him and his wife Margaret jointly between 7 and 12 June 1308: grants of land in perpetuity or for life, grants of free warren, etc.[13] Since some of these grants were made to compensate the former earl and countess of Cornwall for the loss of revenue from their Cornish estates now forfeit and to ensure their sustenance (to the tune of no less than 6,000 marks sterling a year), it is hardly surprising that the relevant documents should not refer to Gaveston as earl of Cornwall; one of them, however, the grant for life of the county of Gaure and of other lands in Guyenne, goes further and describes Gaveston as 'dilectum et fidelem nostrum Petrum de Gavaston', militem', thus reducing him to the knightly rank which he had held from 26 May 1306 until his elevation to the earldom of Cornwall on 6 August 1307.[14]

The contrast between the wording of a charter by which Gaveston granted to the king the two Berkshire manors of Crookham and Leckhampstead, and that of the subsequent royal charter which regranted him the two manors, provides another illuminating example of baronial control over chancery drafting. In his charter to the king, dated 19 May in London (one day later than the royal letters patent, dated 18 May in Westminster, which sanctioned his exile), Gaveston styled himself 'Petrus de Gavaston', comes Cornubie', whereas the royal charter which regranted the two manors to him on the following 9 June described him simply as 'dilecto et fideli nostro Petro de Gavaston' '.[15] It is virtually certain that Gaveston's charter of 19 May was drafted and written by its last and only clerical witness, Thomas de Newhay, the clerk of Edward II's wardrobe who had written the charter of 6 August 1307.[16]

His clash with the chancery over the comparatively minor matter of Gaveston's comital title had convinced the king that, on more

---

[12] *Vita*, p. 4. [13] PRO C 53/94, m. 6 (*CChR* iii. 110–11).
[14] *Foedera*: R. II. i. 48–9; *CPR 1307–1313*, p. 78.
[15] PRO C 54/125, m. 5d (*CCR 1307–1313*, p. 65); above, n. 13.
[16] PRO E 41/460; Chaplais, *ERD*, pl. 8*b* and n.; J. H. Hodson, 'Medieval Charters: The Last Witness', *Journal of the Society of Archivists*, 5/2 (1974), 71–89 and nn.

substantial points such as his adoptive brother's future in general and his place of exile in particular, he could not hope for great seal letters to be issued, if at all, in a form of his own choice as long as the seal remained in London under baronial control. One alternative he had was to get hold of the great seal and supervise in person the drafting and sealing of the documents which he had in mind. Some time in the second week of June, the chancellor visited the king in King's Langley. Although, at their meeting, the two men may have discussed more than one topic, it cannot be doubted that the question of letters for Gaveston was high on the agenda: before they parted, the king ordered the chancellor to send him Adam Osgodby, keeper of the chancery rolls, with the great seal. On his return to London, the chancellor complied and Osgodby duly arrived with the seal in King's Langley on Sunday, 9 June. What use, if any, Edward made of the seal on this occasion is unknown; next morning, Osgodby and his charge were already on their way back to London.[17] Five days later, the chancellor was told by Walter Reynolds that the king wanted the seal again. Langton obeyed once more and the great seal was in the king's hands from Saturday, 15 June until Thursday, 20 June.[18]

On 15 and 16 June letters were issued under the king's direct supervision. Their text is known from their enrolment on two separate schedules, which were in due course stitched on to the chancery rolls of the first year of the king's reign, one on the Patent Roll and the other on the Roman Roll. A note on each of the schedules records that all the documents were read and sealed before the king, and that, by the king's order, the sealing also took place in the presence of one earl, the earl of Richmond, and of Henry de Percy, Hugh le Despenser, William Melton, and Adam Osgodby.[19] All the letters were directly or indirectly connected with the future of Gaveston, whose name, whenever it occurs, is always followed by the title of earl of Cornwall, contrary to the invariable practice of the chancery in London.

The schedule to the Patent Roll begins with the grant of the castle and town of Blanquefort in Guyenne to Bertrand de Got, a nephew of Clement V (16 June). The king's motives for his generosity towards Bertrand are expressed in the document with remarkable

---

[17] *Parl. Writs*, II. ii, app. p. 14.   [18] Ibid.
[19] Ibid., app. p. 15; *Foedera*: R. II. i. 50; *CPR 1307–1313*, p. 83.

candour: Edward was making the grant because he was anxious to please the holy father, who as a result might be all the more ready to be favourably disposed towards his affairs, and because he wished to bind Bertrand to the promotion of whatever royal business might come before the curia.[20] On the very day of the grant, as we shall see, several favours concerning Gaveston were indeed requested from Clement V.

The royal lieutenancy in Ireland

The text of the grant of Blanquefort is followed by subsidiary writs relating to its execution. The other documents on the schedule to the Patent Roll concern the appointment of a royal lieutenant in Ireland. The first, dated 15 June at Reading, appoints Richard de Burgh, earl of Ulster, to the post during the king's pleasure. Next comes the appointment, dated next day, 16 June, also at Reading, apparently to the same post and also during the king's pleasure, of Piers Gaveston, earl of Cornwall. The two commissions are strikingly different in form and contents. Among minor differences, the letters patent appointing Gaveston have a more detailed list of addressees, which mentions specifically the chief justiciar, the chancellor, and the treasurer of Ireland; they also have an additional, preliminary clause announcing that the king is sending Gaveston to Ireland. More important is the clause, absent from the commission to the earl of Ulster, which gives Gaveston full power to remove any royal official in Ireland, whenever necessary, and appoint someone else in his place. An even more distinctive feature of Gaveston's commission is that it is cast in the form of a procuration, although by the fourteenth century this type of commission had largely become obsolete except for the appointment of some particular diplomatic representatives. In this respect it was, *mutatis mutandis*, a replica of Henry II's appointment of William fitz Audelin, the first ever royal lieutenant in Ireland.[21] Edward ordered all archbishops and others in Ireland to obey Gaveston, during his term of office as lieutenant, as they would obey his own person ('tanquam nobis ipsis'), in the same way as Henry II had ordered

---

[20] *Foedera*: R. II. i. 51; *CPR 1307–1313*, p. 83.
[21] Ibid.; *Parl. Writs*, II. ii, app. p. 15; *Recueil des actes de Henri II* . . ., ed. L. Delisle and E. Berger, 4 vols. (Paris, 1909–27), i. 459, no. cccx.

their predecessors to obey William fitz Audelin as they would obey him ('sicut michimet'); Edward gave Gaveston power to take whatever action he would take himself, if he was present ('prout faceremus, si presentes essemus'), just as Henry had said that he would ratify William fitz Audelin's actions as if they were his own deeds ('tanquam egomet fecissem'). Gaveston's commission is followed by two other documents, also dated 16 June: one orders the earl of Ulster to give aid and counsel to Gaveston, and the other gives the latter full power to issue letters of presentation and collation to vacant churches and benefices in Ireland as long as he remains lieutenant there or until the king decides otherwise.[22]

The letters enrolled on the schedule to the Roman Roll are all dated at Windsor on 16 June. Two of them, one addressed to Philip IV and the other to Clement V, relate how, after his accession, Edward had granted the earldom of Cornwall to Gaveston in the latter's absence and without his knowledge, not only with the consent of the earls and barons of the kingdom, but even at their instigation. Latterly, however, the earls and barons had changed their minds and rebelled against the king. As the dispute was likely to expose the kingdom to grave scandals and perils, the king asked Clement and Philip to send to England one or more peace-loving men each to investigate ways of restoring peace within the realm. In another letter, the king begged the pope to revoke the sentence of excommunication which, without admonition, summons, confession, or conviction of any offence, had been pronounced unjustly by the archbishop of Canterbury and the other English bishops against Gaveston, if he did not leave the kingdom by 25 June, from which sentence Gaveston had appealed to the holy see. Three other letters asked respectively the college of cardinals, Otton de Grandson, and Amanieu d'Albret to use their good offices to induce the pope to revoke the sentence.[23]

If we assume that the documents which were sealed with the great seal while it was in the king's hands were all without exception enrolled on the two schedules, no more than thirteen letters were issued during that period, one on 15 June and the rest on the following day. Only the earliest one, the appointment of the earl of Ulster as royal lieutenant in Ireland, poses any real problem. Of all the measures

---

[22] *Parl. Writs*, II. ii, app. p. 15.   [23] *Foedera*: R. II. i. 49–50.

embodied in the great seal documents issued at Reading and Windsor, it was the only one which the baronial council in London had no reason to reject and for which therefore letters patent could have been sealed by the chancery in London quite openly instead of being issued semi-stealthily in Reading. Nobody could have imagined that the appointment of Richard de Burgh might be of advantage to Gaveston, except the king, of course, who, on 15 June, was perhaps thinking of Ireland as a safe haven for his adoptive brother under the protection of a friendly lieutenant, whose daughter Maud and son John were soon to marry respectively Gilbert, earl of Gloucester, and Gilbert's sister Elizabeth, both of whom were related to Gaveston by marriage; the two weddings were celebrated at Waltham, one on 29 September 1308 and the other on the next day.[24] Within twenty-four hours, however, if we take the dates of our documents literally, Ulster's appointment was to all intents and purposes rescinded by Gaveston's commission to the same post. Ireland, yesterday a mere place of refuge for a reluctant exile, was now offered to him as a land of opportunity for authority and power.[25] While Edward was in France in January–February, Gaveston had as *custos regni* issued royal letters sealed with the English great seal of absence under his own attestation; now he would do the same as *locum tenens Hibernie* for royal letters sealed with the great seal of Ireland; for the second time in one year he would authorize the issue of letters which began with the words 'Edward by the grace of God king of England'.[26]

Although it has been assumed above that, because Richard de Burgh had been appointed during the king's pleasure, his commission was automatically made null and void by the subsequent appointment of Gaveston, there is no evidence to show that it was officially cancelled: both appointments are enrolled consecutively on the schedule to the Patent Roll without any indication that they in fact conflicted with one another; the originals may even have been sealed at the same time. We may wonder therefore whether the commission to Richard de Burgh was not kept in reserve in case something went wrong with Gaveston's appointment.

[24] Phillips, *Pembroke*, p. 14; Bodl. Lib. MS Lat. Hist. c. 5, m. 3.
[25] Hamilton, *Gaveston*, pp. 55–7.
[26] For royal seals used in the central administration of Ireland, see *Archaeologia*, 85 (1936), 314–23 and pl. XCI–XCIV; the system of deputed chanceries is briefly described in Chaplais, *ERD*, pp. 45–50.

While he had the great seal in his custody (15–20 June), Edward seems to have used it strictly for the authentication of letters which concerned Gaveston closely, that is to say those enrolled on the two schedules, and for nothing else, honouring perhaps a bargain which he might have struck with Langton and Osgodby. Any other matter which required the issue of great seal letters was referred to the chancery in London by privy seal warrant, even if the letters had been requested by Gaveston, in which case, as before 15 June, the mention of the title of earl of Cornwall in the warrant was omitted by the chancery. This is true of the grant, which has been cited earlier, to the royal clerk Roger de Clotherum of the smaller piece of the seal for recognizances in the city of York.[27] Since in this example, as was the normal but not invariable practice of the period, the place-date and time-date of the great seal letters patent (Newbury, 18 June) were copied from the privy seal warrant, neither the date of receipt of the warrant nor the date of sealing of the letters in chancery can be established, although the sealing cannot have taken place before 20 June, the day on which Osgodby returned the great seal to the chancellor in London, some time after 3 p.m.[28]

According to the *Annales Paulini*, Gaveston sailed from Bristol to Ireland on 28 June 1308, the eve of the feast of St Peter and St Paul,[29] three days after the date set in the excommunication sentence of 24 May, which had therefore become effective *ipso facto*.[30] He returned to England almost exactly one year later, sailing from Ireland, according to the Irish Annals, on 23 June 1309, the eve of the Nativity of St John the Baptist,[31] two days before the expiry of his letters of protection, which had been issued on 25 June 1308 to last for one year.[32] What we know for certain is that he arrived in Chester, where the king was at the time, on Friday, 27 June 1309.[33] During

---

[27] PRO C 81/60/210; C 66/130, m. 4 (*CPR 1307–1313*, p. 79).

[28] *Parl. Writs*, II. ii, app. p. 14.   [29] *Ann. Paul.*, p. 263.

[30] *Reg. Simonis de Gandavo*, i. 238–40.

[31] *Chartularies of St Mary's Abbey, Dublin*, ed. J. T. Gilbert, ii (RS, 1884), 294 (Annals of Ireland).

[32] *CPR 1307–1313*, p. 80 (John Charlton is named first in the list of those who obtained protections on the same day; ibid.).

[33] *Vita*, p. 7; Bodl. Lib. MS Lat. Hist. c. 5, m. 10, under date Friday, 27 June 1309: 'Rex apud Cestr'. Isto die venit comes Cornubie usque Cestr'; Maddicott, *Lancaster*, p. 103; Phillips, *Pembroke*, p. 29.

Gaveston's stay in Ireland, the childish game between the king and the chancery over the title of earl of Cornwall went on unabated. Gaveston, for his part, described himself consistently as 'earl of Cornwall, lieutenant of our lord the king in Ireland'.[34] Edward also continued to give him the comital title, for example in two privy seal writs issued at Woodstock on 5 July 1308.[35] As mentioned earlier, one of these writs called him further 'nostre cher frere et feal' and the other 'nostre feal et loial': in Edward's eyes the compact of adoptive brotherhood which he had contracted with Gaveston some years earlier was still very much in force; nor was his adoptive brother's loyalty to be doubted in spite of the allegation made in the articles of April 1308 that he was 'a traitor to his liege lord and to the realm'.[36] Meanwhile, the policy of the chancery remained unchanged until 5 August 1309, when the earldom of Cornwall was restored to Gaveston.[37] For example, in great seal letters patent of 15 May 1309, which granted to Gaveston the custody of the lands of four deceased tenants-in-chief in Yorkshire while their heirs were under age, the grantee is referred to by name only, without any title.[38] One apparent exception has been noted, a great seal letter dated 13 April 1309 at Grovebury and enrolled on the Roman Roll: in this letter Edward thanks Raymond de Got, cardinal deacon of S. Maria Nova, for interceding with Philip the Fair on behalf of Gaveston, who is here given the title of earl of Cornwall.[39] But it is probable that, according to a practice not uncommon for diplomatic correspondence under the great seal, the letter was brought to the chancery ready for sealing, having been drafted and written in the wardrobe, whose controller, William Melton, was also keeper of the privy seal. Melton certainly seems to have visited the chancery on 13 April, since on that day another great seal letter was issued, also at Grovebury, following an oral message which he had brought in from the king ('per ipsum

---

[34] *Calendar of Ormond Deeds*, ed. Edmund Curtis, i (Dublin, 1932), no. 438; *Calendar of the Justiciary Rolls . . . of Ireland, 1–7 Edw. II* (Dublin, [1952]), p. 84; *Historic and Municipal Documents of Ireland, AD 1172–1320*, ed. J. T. Gilbert (RS, 1870), p. 230; *Rotulorum patentium et clausorum Cancellariae Hiberniae Calendarium*, I. i (Rec. Comm., 1828), 7; J. S. Hamilton, 'Edward II and the Murage of Dublin . . .', *Documenting the Past: Essays in Medieval History presented to G. P. Cuttino*, ed. J. S. Hamilton and Patricia J. Bradley (Woodbridge, 1989), p. 95.

[35] PRO C 81/60/258 (*Cal. Chanc. War.* i. 276); above, ch. 1 n. 33.

[36] Richardson and Sayles, *The Governance of Mediaeval England*, p. 468; *Bridlington*, p. 34.

[37] *CChR* iii. 131.   [38] *Foedera*: R. II. i. 73.   [39] Ibid. 71.

regem, nunciante W. de Melton').[40] We may note in passing that a letter of 4 September 1309 to Clement V is said to have been given under the privy seal, although, like the letter to Raymond de Got, it is enrolled on the Roman Roll and should therefore have been sealed with the great seal.[41]

If the grant of Blanquefort to Bertrand de Got on 16 June 1308 was meant to be an inducement to Clement V to grant the king's request of the same date to revoke the sentence of excommunication against Gaveston, it did not have the desired effect. The pope explained later that, although he had been anxious to obviate any scandal affecting the king and his kingdom, he had at the time decided, for some (undisclosed) reasons, not to take any action, apart from appointing Master Hugues Géraud, precentor of the church of Périgueux, to hear Gaveston's appeal against the sentence.[42]

It was not until the spring of 1309 that the pope agreed to revoke the sentence and absolve Gaveston. He had changed his mind, he said in the revocation bull, for two reasons. In the first place, the king had recently written to him that the dissensions in the kingdom had been resolved and that the earls and barons responsible for the exile and excommunication of Gaveston now regretted their error and were eager for him to return. In the second place, Gaveston, through Bertrand Caillau, his proctor, had argued that the sentence was null because he had appealed against it before 25 June, the date set for its enforcement.[43]

The embassy to Avignon

The recent letters of Edward to which the pope referred were probably delivered by the bishops of Worcester and Norwich, the earls of Richmond and Pembroke, and the other members of the solemn embassy which, soon after 15 March 1309,[44] left England for Avignon with royal letters of credence dated eleven days earlier.[45] From a papal letter addressed to Edward on 26 May we learn that the envoys did indeed deliver to the pope on the king's behalf, not only an

[40] *Gascon Rolls*, iv, ed. Y. Renouard, no. 243.   [41] *Foedera*: R. II. i. 88.
[42] *Reg. Simonis de Gandavo*, i. 315.
[43] Ibid. See *Corpus Juris Canonici, Decret. Greg.* II. xxviii. 40.
[44] See *Cal. Chanc. War.* i. 283.   [45] *Foedera*: R. II. i. 69.

oral message ('proposuerunt'), but also letters, in all probability those to which the pope alluded in his bull of absolution and not the embassy's letters of credence of 4 March, which were, as usual, quite uninformative;[46] the pope also says that petitions were presented to him by the envoys *ad exaudicionis graciam*,[47] a phrase which, although it belongs to the vocabulary of the papal chancery,[48] occurs in one but only one of the embassy's two royal letters of credence. The first of these two letters tells the pope that Walter Reynolds, bishop of Worcester, John Salmon, bishop of Norwich, John of Brittany, earl of Richmond, Aymer de Valence, earl of Pembroke, Boniface of Saluzzo, archdeacon of Buckingham, Otton de Grandson, Amanieu d'Albret, and Robert fitz Payn, steward of the household, will explain to him fully some matters touching the king, and asks that credence be given to them (or to seven, six, five, four, three, or two of them).[49] In the second letter only two names are mentioned, those of Walter Reynolds and John of Brittany, who are to inform the pope in secret of some matters of particular concern to the king; the letter begs the pope to admit the bishop and the earl *ad exaudicionis graciam*, in other words, to grant the petitions to be presented by them in the king's name, and to give credence to them as to the king's mouthpiece ('sicut organo vocis nostre').[50]

Although there is no surviving record of the messages given to the pope either openly by the whole embassy or in private by the bishop of Worcester and the earl of Richmond, we may unhesitatingly assume that the secret information and the petitions presented *ad exaudicionis graciam* concerned Gaveston. It was no accident that the two envoys selected to deliver the confidential message and the petitions were respectively the members of the episcopate and higher nobility who

---

[46] The pope's letter is printed in *Foedera*: R. II. i. 75; see also Zutshi, *Original Papal Letters in England, 1305–1415*, no. 61.   [47] *Foedera*: R. II. i. 75.

[48] See E. Perroy, *L'Angleterre et le grand schisme d'Occident* (Paris, 1933), p. 414 (letter from Boniface IX to Richard II); compare *The Diplomatic Correspondence of Richard II*, ed. E. Perroy (Royal Historical Society, Camden 3rd Series, xlviii, 1933), nos. 97, 118. The phrase 'ad exaudicionis graciam' seems always to have been connected with the presentation of petitions.

[49] *Foedera*: R. II. i. 69.

[50] Ibid. See Kathleen Edwards, 'The Political Importance of English Bishops during the Reign of Edward II', *EHR* 59 (1944), 317; Chaplais, *EMDP* I. i. 52–3 n. 17. Since the words 'ad exaudicionis graciam' only occur in the letters of credence of Reynolds and Richmond, it follows that they were to present on their own the petitions (concerning Gaveston) to the pope. The other envoys (among them the bishop of Norwich and the earl of Pembroke) were excluded.

had shown themselves to be most consistently loyal to the king and friendly towards Gaveston. When Edward came to the throne, Walter Reynolds had already served him faithfully for no less than ten years in his household and wardrobe. His continued loyalty was to bring him substantial rewards both in the civil service (first as treasurer and later as chancellor) and in the Church (first as bishop of Worcester and later as archbishop of Canterbury).[51] The high regard which Edward had for Reynolds was so well known in the curia that it was to him that on several occasions the pope turned for assistance in his dealings with the king.[52] Cryptic references in the accounts of the royal wardrobe to letters sent by 'the treasurer' to Ponthieu on 16 and 17 July 1307, and to letters from the king to Gaveston being delivered at the London house of Reynolds on 19 July, suggest that the future bishop of Worcester took more than a passing interest in Gaveston's return from exile at the beginning of the reign.[53]

The earl of Richmond for his part had been the only earl to witness three charters for Gaveston issued on 9, 10, and 12 June 1308.[54] He was also the only earl present when, on 15 and 16 June, letters close and patent, all of them connected in one way or another with Gaveston's future, were sealed with the great seal before the king.[55] Gaveston loved Richmond, according to the latter's chaplain, 'beyond measure', a phrase which chroniclers were fond of applying to the king's feelings for his adoptive brother, and in their correspondence Gaveston and the earl called one another father and son.[56]

If Reynolds and Richmond were the only envoys privy to the king's secret message to the pope and if this was the only message connected with Gaveston, we should be wary of interpreting the participation of the earl of Pembroke in the embassy as an indubitable proof that in March 1309 he was on the side of the king and Gaveston, although

---

[51] For the career of Reynolds, see J. Robert Wright, *The Church and the English Crown, 1305–1334* (Toronto, 1980), pp. 243–74; John Le Neve, *Fasti Ecclesiae Anglicanae, 1300–1541*, iv (Monastic Cathedrals), comp. B. Jones (Athlone Press, London, 1963), pp. 3, 55; Tout, *Chapters*, vi. 379.

[52] Zutshi, *Original Papal Letters in England, 1305–1415*, nos. 52, 57, 63.

[53] PRO E 101/373/15, fos. 23ʳ, 25ʳ.

[54] PRO C 53/94, m. 6 (*CChR* iii. 110).

[55] *Foedera*: R. II. i. 50; *Parl. Writs*, II. ii, app. p. 15.

[56] Below, App. I. 3. I know of no evidence which supports this statement: in a letter dated 2 Mar. [1311] in Dundee, Gaveston simply calls Richmond, his correspondent, 'trescher cosin' (PRO SC 1/49/169; I. Lubimenko, *Jean de Bretagne, comte de Richmond* (Lille, 1908), p. 141).

this may well have been the case.[57] For the general change of heart of the earls and barons at that date our only evidence is Edward's (written) word as reported by the pope in the bull of revocation of Gaveston's excommunication.

The bishop of Worcester and the earl of Richmond were still in England on 15 March. They probably were the bearers of the privy seal writ, issued on that day from King's Langley, which informed the chancellor that they would call to collect the great seal documents which they and their fellow-envoys required for their mission to the pope.[58] They could not therefore have sailed from Dover to Wissant much before 18 March. A solemn embassy such as theirs would travel at a more leisurely pace than couriers, who in the 1320s were allowed fifteen days to cover the distance from Wissant to Avignon.[59] In addition, the embassy had been instructed to deliver an oral message to the king of France on its way to the papal curia.[60] This was bound to add at least a couple of days to its travelling-time and make its arrival in Avignon before the beginning of the second week of April most unlikely.

The envoys stayed in Avignon for some weeks. They certainly were still there on 15 May, the date of a grant which they made on the king's behalf to Raymond Guillaume de Budos, a nephew of Clement V: the grant is recorded in letters patent made out in the names of the bishop of Worcester and of the earls of Richmond and Pembroke, and the witnesses present included the bishop of Norwich and the other envoys for whom letters of credence addressed to Clement V and Philip IV had been issued on 4 March, except Otton de Grandson, who perhaps had in any case been prevented from joining in the mission.[61] It is likely that the embassy took its official leave of the pope shortly after 26 May. On that day Clement wrote to Edward a

[57] Maddicott, *Lancaster*, pp. 94–5; Phillips, *Pembroke*, p. 29.
[58] *Cal. Chanc. War.* i. 283.   [59] Chaplais, *EMDP* i. ii. 765.
[60] *Foedera*: R. II. i. 68 (letters of credence addressed to Philip IV and dated 4 Mar.). If it is to this mission that the *Annales Paulini* refer (*Ann. Paul.*, p. 266), Reynolds and his colleagues called on the king of France to present their master's apologies for his inability to visit France and attend a meeting which Philip IV, in his efforts to mediate between England and Scotland, wished to arrange between Edward, Robert Bruce, and himself.
[61] *Gascon Rolls*, iv, ed. Renouard, no. 260; *Foedera*: R. II. i. 72–3. The 'quorum' clause in the letters of credence of the whole embassy allowed for all the named envoys except two to drop out. It is clear, although not specified in this instance, that the two were to be Reynolds and Richmond.

letter typical of the *littere responsorie* which every embassy about to
return home expected to be given by its host for delivery to its sender:
the letter begins with an acknowledgement of the embassy's visit and of
the receipt of the king's letters, petitions, and oral messages brought
by the envoys, who will convey the pope's answer to the king; it ends
with the statement of the pope's intention to send shortly to England
special envoys of his own in connection with matters of special
concern to both himself and the king.[62]

The papal bull of absolution

The papal bull revoking the sentence of excommunication against
Gaveston is supposed to have been issued on 25 April (*vii kal. maii*)
1309, that is to say within two or three weeks of the probable arrival
of Reynolds and Richmond in Avignon.[63] Although this date has
never been challenged, a later one *c.*21 May would unquestionably
make better sense. Since Gaveston could not safely return from exile
until he had been absolved by the pope and his absolution made
known to the English bishops and earls responsible for the excommunication, we may take it for granted that the king would have
instructed his envoys to send him the papal bull by courier as soon as
it had been obtained and that he would have informed Archbishop
Winchelsey of its contents immediately after its arrival. If the bull was
really issued on 25 April and we allow two days for possible delays in
its delivery to the envoys, an express messenger might have left
Avignon with it on 27 April, reaching the king before 15 May. We
would have expected the archbishop to be given the terms of the bull
in the next few days, instead of which he was asked by privy seal letter
to appear before the king in London on 9 June, more than three weeks
after the presumed arrival of the bull, a delay uncharacteristic of
Edward in a matter of such vital importance for Gaveston's return. In
fact, the archbishop, pleading illness, did not present himself until two
days later, 11 June, on which day, at the king's command, the bull
was recited to him.[64] Although the date of Edward's privy seal

---

[62] *Foedera*: R. II. i. 75; Zutshi, *Original Papal Letters in England, 1305–1415*, no. 61.

[63] *Reg. Simonis de Gandavo*, i. 314–16; *Reg. Ricardi de Swinfield*, pp. 451–2.

[64] *Reg. Simonis de Gandavo*, i. 313–14. The *Annales Paulini* wrongly state that the papal bull was
brought to London from Avignon by the bishop of Norwich about the feast of St John the Baptist
(24 June; *Ann. Paul.*, p. 267).

summons is not known, we should probably place it, as well as the date of arrival of the papal bull in England, towards the end of the first week in June, in which case the bull is likely to have been issued, not on 25 April, but three or four weeks later, a week or so before the envoys left Avignon to return to England. There is, of course, no reason why the bull of absolution for Gaveston should have been issued at the same time as the other bulls which the envoys obtained for the king and others as well as for themselves. It is worth noting, however, that, apart from an indult for a portable altar granted to the earl of Richmond on 7 May,[65] all the other bulls which seem to have been issued as the result of the envoys' visit are dated between 21 and 27 May:[66] those dated 21 May (*xii kal. junii*) include three for the king, the originals of which are still extant, two for Queen Isabella, and ten for (or at the request of) Walter Reynolds.[67] All the known texts of the bull of absolution are dated 25 April (*vii kal. maii*),[68] but they all are ultimately derived from a Canterbury text, which may have been taken either directly from the original, which was in the king's hands, or, perhaps more plausibly, from a copy due to a royal scribe, who may have read the date of the original as *vii kal. maii* in error for *xii kal. junii*.

Whatever the true date of the bull of absolution may have been, its provisions were not quite as satisfactory as the two adoptive brothers might have wished. It was a bull of absolution *ad cautelam* only:[69] the sentence of excommunication was truly annulled and Gaveston could return from Ireland without fear of being arrested by the barons as an excommunicate; but the annulment was granted merely for procedural reasons, namely because Gaveston had appealed from the sentence before it was due to come into force, not because the sentence had been unjust. On this last point it would be for the judges of appeal to decide, and Bertrand Caillau, Gaveston's proctor in the curia, had in advance sworn in his principal's name to observe the court's decision.[70] If the appeal failed and the grounds on which the sentence

[65] *CPL* ii. 50.   [66] *CPL* ii. 52–8.

[67] Zutshi, *Original Papal Letters in England, 1305–1415*, nos. 58–60; *CPL* ii. 52, 53, 55.

[68] *Reg. Simonis de Gandavo*, i. 314–16; *Reg. Ricardi de Swinfield*, pp. 451–2; *Historical MSS Commission Reports*, VIII, app. i. 352.

[69] *Reg. Simonis de Gandavo*, i. 315–16. See *Corpus Juris Canonici, Decret. Greg.* v. xxxix. 52; F. Donald Logan, *Excommunication and the Secular Arm in Mediaeval England* (Toronto, 1968), pp. 118–20.   [70] *Reg. Simonis de Gandavo*, i. 316.

of excommunication had been passed were found to have been just, Gaveston could be excommunicated again. To this possibility the king did not react until 4 September 1309, the date of a privy seal letter in which he thanked the pope for the bull of absolution, begging him at the same time to release Gaveston from the oath which Caillau had taken in his name.[71]

From the complete silence of English chronicles on Gaveston's deeds in Ireland it may not be unreasonable to infer that his lieutenancy was regarded in England neither as a spectacular success nor as a complete disgrace. The only comment in the *Vita* is that, with the king's authorization, the lieutenant had squandered for his own use all the king's revenues in the land, probably a gratuitous remark which can be neither proved nor disproved.[72] What is perhaps more important is that Gaveston's removal from the English scene had brought no improvement to the government of the kingdom. The holding of the Dunstable tournament at the end of March or beginning of April 1309 and the text of the grievances presented to the king at the parliament which met on 27 April show that, at the time, the commons were just as disaffected as the earls and barons.[73] Perhaps there were some among those who framed the grievances, particularly among the members of the commons, who were beginning to wonder how far Gaveston was to blame for all the evil which had gone on in royal administration. Writing to an exile, who, although anonymous, should almost certainly be identified as Gaveston, at a date unknown but probably to be placed in the latter part of Gaveston's Irish exile, Bishop Henry Woodlock of Winchester reported: 'Your friends are very much on the increase in the parts where we are, and your enemies on the decrease, praise be to the Lord, and with God's help we hope to speak with you face to face in England before long.'[74] Since the bishop goes on to hint at his fear that his letter might fall into enemy hands, as some of his earlier correspondence with the addressee appeared to have done, it is unlikely that he would have provoked the opposition unnecessarily by

---

[71] *Foedera*: R. II. i. 88.

[72] *Vita*, p. 6. But the Annals of Ireland, the reliability of which is not in doubt, praise Gaveston's military achievements; see Conway Davies, *Baron. Opp.*, p. 86; Hamilton, *Gaveston*, pp. 58, 149 nn. 28–9.   [73] Maddicott, *Lancaster*, pp. 95–102.

[74] *Reg. Henrici Woodlock*, ii. 689. See Kathleen Edwards in *EHR* 59 (1944), 322.

telling lies about Gaveston's recently acquired popularity. That there had been a swing of public opinion in Gaveston's favour while he was in Ireland is in any case unexpectedly confirmed by two remarkable letters extant amongst the muniments of Westminster Abbey.[75]

A change of heart in Westminster Abbey

During the period 1307-8 Gaveston had made a mortal enemy of the Westminster monk Brother Roger de Aldenham, the outspoken defender of the convent's liberties, by getting involved in the affairs of the abbey twice in rapid succession, both times for profit (or so Aldenham believed). First he had taken sides with the autocratic abbot, Walter de Wenlok, against the prior, Reginald de Hadham, in the matter of compositions for the division of goods between the abbot and the convent. Accused by the prior and part of the convent, including Aldenham, of having violated the compositions, Wenlok took his revenge on the prior by excommunicating him and suspending him from office in the summer of 1307. Hence various appeals made by Hadham. This first dispute was still in full swing at the end of 1307 when Wenlok's death on 25 December caused a second conflict to erupt in the abbey, this time over the election of Wenlok's successor. The supporters of Wenlok in the first dispute managed to have one of them, the disreputable Richard de Kedyngton, elected by compromise on 26 January 1308. Now they wished to have the election confirmed, while other monks wanted it quashed.[76] In this second dispute Gaveston sided with Kedyngton, whereas Aldenham was in the opposite camp, naming the prior as one of four possible candidates for Wenlok's succession.[77]

The only evidence for Gaveston's interference in the affairs of

---

[75] See below, App. I. 2-3.

[76] On these two disputes, see E. H. Pearce, *Walter de Wenlok, Abbot of Westminster* (London, SPCK, 1920), pp. 167-225; Harvey, *Wenlok*, pp. 17-24.

[77] WAM 5460, m. 1, lines 35-7: below, App. I. 1. Aldenham's three other candidates were Henry de Bircheston, Guy de Ashwell, and Philip de Sutton (see Pearce, *Walter de Wenlok*, pp. 219-20). WAM 5460 is a parchment roll of two membranes, written on the face and on the dorse, in a hand which seems to be nearly contemporary. It contains copies of letters not only from Aldenham, but also from Walter de Bolton, his fellow proctor in the papal curia, and from various other persons connected with Westminster Abbey, nearly all of whom are unnamed and not easy to identify. The text is difficult and corrupt at times. For convenience, references are given to the lines of each membrane of the roll.

Westminster Abbey consists of one letter and complementary schedules written by Aldenham, probably in May or June 1308, while he was in Avignon, acting as one of the proctors of the anti-Kedyngton party.[78] Aldenham recounts how, in the first dispute, when Wenlok realized that the prior wished to prosecute his case against him, he became so afraid that his misdeeds might come out into the open that he contacted Gaveston and gave him £200 as well as innumerable presents. Gaveston in return assumed the defence of Wenlok against Hadham, using his influence with 'the king who now is' to prevent the prior from having his grievances heard, supporting the abbot *usque ad mortem* against God and the truth, and having some of the monks sent into exile. After the death of Wenlok, his accomplices succeeded in having one of them elected as abbot; that was Richard de Kedyngton, a man described by Aldenham as 'illiteratum, irreligiosum, in omnibus insufficientem, diversis crimini-bus et infamiis fornicacionis et adulterii irretitum'. After the king had twice declined to assent to the election because of the ill repute of the abbot-elect, Kedyngton's accomplices got in touch with Gaveston, as Wenlok had done, and gave him £100 out of the money left by the late abbot. Whereupon Gaveston arranged for the king to confirm the election and for letters supporting Kedyngton to be sent by the king and queen to the pope and cardinals, and to the king of France. Aldenham's suggested riposte was that, among others, the queen and the earl of Lincoln should be secretly approached through suitable intermediaries and told the true facts about Kedyngton's character and Gaveston's campaign of misinformation on Kedyngton's behalf. As both the queen and the earl hated Gaveston to the death, it should not be difficult to persuade them to forward the correct information to the pope and cardinals and to the king of France and Charles de Valois, all of whom were unaware of Kedyngton's unworthiness and of Gaveston's involvement; sharing as they did the same hatred of Gaveston, they would be delighted to hinder him and those connected with him.[79] Amongst other things, the earl of Lincoln should be told that, at the instigation of the abbot-elect and at the request of Gaveston, some members of the convent had been imprisoned; both

---

[78] Below, App. I. 1. See Maddicott, *Lancaster*, pp. 84–6.
[79] WAM 5460, m. 1, lines 1–55, 82–185; below, App. I. 1.

Gaveston and Kedyngton had also procured or intended to procure letters asking the king of France to have Aldenham arrested.[80]

Time and time again, Aldenham stresses that Gaveston, to whom he refers once as 'the accursed Peter' ('Petri maledicti'), sided with Wenlok and Kedyngton after being bribed by them ('pro pecunia' or 'per corrupcionem munerum'), and that he had supported their falsehoods knowingly ('fraudulenter' or 'falsa procuracione'). On the strength of the documentary evidence available, neither of these two charges can be substantiated or refuted. There is no trace of a gift of £200 to Gaveston in the accounts of Wenlok's receiver, Brother Henry Payn, which have happily survived for the crucial period 13 December 1305–24 December 1307.[81] This is not surprising, of course, since out of his net annual income of about £520 as abbot,[82] Wenlok could hardly have afforded to spend £200 on a bribe to Gaveston. Nor was he likely to have been able to charge to the larger account of the convent, whose net annual income amounted to about £1,100,[83] an expenditure designed to bring about the prior's downfall. If the sum of £200 was really given to Gaveston and if it was a bribe, the abbot must have paid it out of his own private funds, not out of the income for which his own receiver or the conventual treasurer accounted. The same may be said of the £100 allegedly given to Gaveston by Kedyngton's supporters out of the £1,000 which they acquired from the estate of the late abbot.

On at least two occasions Gaveston did receive presents from Wenlok, but they were not extravagant: in Edward I's reign, at the end of November 1306, it was a cash payment of £6. 13s. 4d., that is to say 10 marks; at the beginning of the next reign, in October 1307, it was a gift of one gilt cup, one gilt jug, and another small jug, the first two of these three items having cost the abbot £10. 12s. 0d.[84] There was nothing unusual or suspicious about these gifts. In 1305, when Walter Reynolds was keeper of Edward of Carnarvon's wardrobe, he was granted by Wenlok an annuity of 10 marks for life.[85] Other small gifts were made from time to time to various royal officials, for

---

[80] WAM 5460, m. 1, lines 119–21; below, App. I. 1.

[81] Harvey, *Wenlok*, pp. 195–214.

[82] Barbara Harvey, *Westminster Abbey and its Estates in the Middle Ages* (Oxford, 1977), p. 63.

[83] Ibid.   [84] Harvey, *Wenlok*, I, no. 227, and pp. 201, 212.

[85] Ibid., p. 32 and n. 13.

instance to three *camerarii* of King Edward I, to the criers of the courts of the king's bench and common pleas, etc.[86] It was no doubt understood that the recipients of such gifts would look after the abbot's interests within their power; in one particular case, that of the two clerks Adam and Richard, the first of whom received 10s. as clerk of the steward of the king's household and the second 3s. 4d. as clerk of the marshal of the same department, Henry Payn states in his account that the gifts had been made 'pro libertate domini favorabilius salvanda'.[87] He does not unfortunately make any comment at all when he records the abbot's gifts to Gaveston. Were these gifts made to him as the holder of some particular office in the administration of Edward of Carnarvon before and after his accession to the throne, or simply as the person most intimate with Edward? If we look carefully at the references to the two gifts in Henry Payn's accounts and in the writs of Wenlok which ordered the first one to be made, we notice that in each case the present to Gaveston is followed by a smaller one to John Charlton: in the first instance 20s. to Charlton for £6. 13s. 4d. to Gaveston, and in the second, one gilt goblet with a lid to Charlton for one gilt cup and two gilt jugs to Gaveston.[88] It was no accident that on a third occasion Charlton alone received a gift: the abbot's writ ordering the payment of 20s. to him is dated 24 April 1307,[89] only six days before the date by which Gaveston was to leave England for his first exile and thus not only lose for an indefinite period all his influence at court, but even become totally irrelevant to the country's politics.[90] Nor can it be by accident that in the diatribes of Aldenham's letters of May or June 1308 the names of Gaveston and Charlton are inextricably linked. It was at the instigation and request of Gaveston and his *secretarius* John Charlton that the king and Walter Reynolds, the treasurer, had written daily letters to the papal curia and to the king of France on behalf of Kedyngton. Like Gaveston, Charlton had been bought by bribes ('per corrupcionem munerum').[91] In one passage in which Aldenham claims that Charlton, at the instigation of his nephew, a carter in Westminster, had done much

---

[86] Ibid., I, nos. 178, 188, 245, and pp. 198, 205.
[87] Ibid., p. 212. Compare a cancelled entry which reads: 'Item j cuppa deaurata data marescallo domini regis pro libertate recuperanda' (ibid.).
[88] Ibid., I, no. 227, and pp. 201, 212.   [89] Ibid., I, no. 241, and p. 204.
[90] *Foedera*: R. I. ii. 1010; Hamilton, *Gaveston*, pp. 34–6.
[91] WAM 5460, m. 2, line 4; below, App. I. 1.

harm to the abbey, he describes him not only as Gaveston's *secretarius* 'from the beginning', but also as *camerarius*, that is to say as royal chamberlain, the earliest reference we have to his holding that post.[92] If, Aldenham continues, the queen and the earl of Lincoln knew what sort of man Charlton was, they would find a way of having him removed from office.[93]

Perhaps there might be some truth after all in the allegation made by some chroniclers that Gaveston was Edward's chamberlain before and after 7 July 1307; perhaps he was the titular chamberlain and Charlton acted as his deputy, in the same way as the earl of Warwick never acted in person as chamberlain of the exchequer, but did so through a deputy appointed by him.[94] The Wenlok gifts to Gaveston would have been made to him as the titular head of Edward's chamber and those to Charlton as the acting deputy.

Whatever we may think of the charges of corruption levelled at Gaveston, we have no reason to doubt that Roger de Aldenham believed them to be true. The war against Kedyngton and his supporters had to be waged by every means conceivable; this was the aim of Aldenham and of his 'lord' (*dominus meus*) and adviser in the papal curia, Thomas Jorz, the 'English cardinal', but the fight against the lies of the enemies had to be conducted by exposing them and forwarding to the right people the correct information according to the truth.[95]

The news of Gaveston's departure for Ireland in June 1308 must

---

[92] WAM 5460, m. 2, line 6; below, App. I. 1. The earliest date suggested by Conway Davies (*Baron. Opp.*, p. 216 n. 4) and Tout (*Chapters*, ii. 225 n. 1) for Charlton's chamberlainship [or deputy chamberlainship] was 23 Feb. [1310], the date of the following entry from an Issue Roll of the exchequer (PRO E 403/150, m. 11): 'Eidem xxiij° die februarii, lx li. liberat' domino Johanni de Cherleton', militi camer' domini regis, de prestito super eo quod ei debetur de garderoba dicti domini regis in una tallia facta Hugoni de Croft', vicecomiti Salop' et Staff' de remanenti compoti sui per literam acquietancie ipsius domini Johannis recepcionem dicte pecunie testificantem in custodia camer' remanentem per preceptum thesaurarii'. Conway Davies, who found this entry, and Tout were uncertain whether the abbreviated *camer'* in *militi camer'* stood for *camerario* or *camere*. There is little doubt, however, that in this instance *camerario* is more likely, since the phrase *in custodia camer'* in the same entry certainly stands for *in custodia camerariorum*, that is to say 'in the custody of the chamberlains' (of the exchequer). It has been noted already that Charlton headed the list of those for whom protections were issued on 25 June 1308 before they left for Ireland in Gaveston's retinue (*CPR 1307–1313*, p. 80; above, n. 32). Aldenham's letter proves that he was already royal chamberlain before that date.
[93] WAM 5460, m. 2, line 8; below, App. I. 1.
[94] Tout, *Place of Edw. II*, pp. 44–5.
[95] WAM 5460, m. 1, lines 20–8; below, App. I. 1.

have been greeted with considerable relief and satisfaction in the anti-Kedyngton camp at Westminster and in Avignon, but disappointment was soon to follow. Gaveston's exile had not brought about any appreciable difference to the case for or against the confirmation of the Westminster election in Avignon. As the king, like everyone else, was getting tired of the delay in the curia, he wrote to the pope on 15 December (by which time Gaveston had been out of England for six months) that, if there were any reasons for which Kedyngton should not be confirmed as abbot, Brother William de Chalk would be a suitable alternative.[96] By Prior Hadham, however, as well as by Aldenham and all those who opposed Kedyngton, the choice of Chalk, a former friend of Wenlok and a supporter of the abbot-elect, could scarcely have been regarded as an improvement.[97] Aldenham also found that the enemies he had made in his fight against Wenlok and the abbot-elect were as powerful as ever in spite of Gaveston's absence. Now they had lodged false accusations against him and he was in trouble with the king and with some of the magnates. Thus it came about, quite incredibly, that both Hadham and Aldenham decided to appeal for help to their former arch-enemy, Gaveston himself. As in the case of the earlier proposed appeal to the queen and to the earl of Lincoln in May or June 1308, Gaveston was to be approached not directly, but *per interpositas personas*, through well-chosen intermediaries. This we learn from the two remarkable letters to which we have referred earlier, one from Hadham and the other from Aldenham.[98] The letter from Hadham has no date at all, but it probably belongs to the latter part of Gaveston's Irish exile. It is addressed to the prior's 'dearest friend' Master Walter Islip, who was royal treasurer in Ireland while Gaveston was lieutenant there, and whose name suggests a family connection with the Westminster manor of Islip in Oxfordshire. After explaining in a few words how Aldenham had been unjustly accused at the instigation of enemies, Hadham begs Islip to approach Gaveston and ask him to send *littere*

[96] *Cal. Chanc. War.* i. 280 (see also 281).

[97] See Aldenham's comment in WAM 5460, m. 1, lines 183–5: 'Electus et fautores sui dicunt in curia quod, si ipse non possit confirmari, W. de Chal' veniet cum tanta potestate litterarum quod omni modo erit abbas noster, quod non credo adhuc istud, et suggeratis comiti quod ipsi omni modo et per omnem viam insistunt per procuracionem Petri virum [*reading uncertain*: unum *or* virum] diffamatum de secta sua nobis preficere in abbatem.'

[98] Below, App. I.

deprecatorie to the king, requesting him to remit all rancour towards Aldenham.[99]

The letter from Aldenham, addressed to his friends in Westminster Abbey, particularly Ralph (de Mordon) and Guy (de Ashwell), was written in Avignon on a Trinity Sunday. Although the year is not stated, from internal evidence the document can safely be assigned to 1309; the full date of the letter must therefore be Sunday, 25 May 1309. The writer does not identify himself, but the substance and style of the letter leave no doubt about his identity. Aldenham tells his correspondents that he knows that his enemies will, either in person or through a special envoy, contact Gaveston as soon as the latter returns to England. They will read to him forged letters, claiming that they come from Aldenham's hand, and they will incite him to urge the king perhaps to write to the papal curia letters hostile to Aldenham. A special friend of Ralph (de Mordon), however, John of Canterbury, chaplain of John of Brittany, earl of Richmond, has told Aldenham that Gaveston is so fond of the earl (in letters they called one another 'father' and 'son') that he will do anything which the earl asks him to do. Would Ralph and Guy do the writer a favour and, as soon as they hear of Gaveston's return, approach the earl through Robert de Haustede or some other friends to induce him to make Gaveston change his mind and stop supporting Aldenham's adversaries? The earl should be told, so that he may pass the information on to Gaveston, of the behaviour and reputation of Brother W(illiam de Chalk, a supporter of Kedyngton), and his accomplices, how they run around like vagrants and fugitives, without their superior's permission, going now to the king, now to the exchequer, now to Ingelard (de Warle), now to the justices and other royal officials, making false accusations, forging letters in the names of Aldenham and others, stirring up trouble against the prior and other good men, etc. If the earl of Richmond is fully informed about all this and if he explains it to Gaveston, the latter will without doubt change his mind completely and turn against Aldenham's enemies, who particularly rely on him, if he returns. Gaveston is unaware of their falsehoods, and he is said to be a man of integrity ('bone consciencie'), when he sees the truth. If he heard the whole story from the earl's mouth, he would no longer

---

[99] WAM 5460, m. 1d, lines 66–73; below, App. I. 2.

listen to the enemies of Aldenham and of the convent. When these
enemies come to see Gaveston, he should tell them neither to rely on
him any more nor to come to see him for such things as in the past. He
should tell them sharply to stay in the cloister, as they ought to do, if
they do not wish something worse to happen to them. Whether
Gaveston returns or not, Aldenham continues (after a few remarks
irrelevant to our story), it would be a good—nay an excellent—thing,
if the earl of Richmond gave the same information to the king, telling
him what a mortal sin it is ('maximum peccatum') to support such
infamous men in their wickedness. The letter ends with the warning:
'Do not lose this letter in the middle of the cloister, as our prior does.'
In an earlier passage of the letter Aldenham had already urged his
correspondents to treat the matters discussed in it with firmness,
discretion, and secrecy.[100]

Aldenham's letter of May 1309, compared with those which he had
written in May or June 1308, shows a complete, unashamed volte-
face on the writer's part. Between 1308 and 1309 he had radically
changed his opinion of Gaveston, who no longer was the accursed
Peter, ready to falsify the truth out of greed, but a man said to be
righteous, who had been misled and was thought to be prepared to
correct his errors, when he was shown the truth.

Within six weeks of his return from Ireland, Gaveston was
regranted the county of Cornwall by a charter dated 5 August 1309 at
Stamford.[101] Apart from a few minor adjustments, the lands granted
in the charter were the same as those in the charter of 6 August 1307.
In both charters the grants were made in perpetuity, but the type of
tenure was different: whereas the charter of 1307 was a grant in fee-
simple to Gaveston and his heirs, that of 1309 was a grant in fee-tail
to Gaveston and his wife, and to the heirs of their bodies. At the same
time, from August 1309, Gaveston regained the title of earl of
Cornwall, which from then until the Ordinances of 1311 was given to
him even by the chancery.[102]

---

[100] WAM 5460, from line 74 of m. 1d to the final line of m. 2d; below, App. I. 3.
[101] CChR iii. 131.
[102] Foedera: R. II. i. 86; CCR 1307–1313, p. 171; CPR 1307–1313, p. 187.

4

LAST EXILE AND DEATH

The Ordinances and Gaveston's indictment

'ONCE he had been reinstated, his behaviour went from bad to worse. He showed his contempt for the earls and barons by giving them vile nicknames. He took offices and dignities from others to bestow them on those close to him. The magnates of the land began to resent this, particularly the earl of Lancaster, because one of his retainers (*familiaribus*) had been removed from office at the instigation of Piers'.[1] These comments in the *Vita*, coming from an author generally and rightly held in high esteem, cannot be dismissed lightly, sceptical though we might feel about their accuracy. For Gaveston to give insulting names to the earls, calling the earl of Warwick, for example, 'the dog of Warwick',[2] was incredibly foolish, but the story and variants of it occur in several other chronicles which do not seem to depend on the *Vita* for their information.[3] Perhaps it was Gaveston's way, admittedly a childish one, of expressing his disappointment and bitterness at being rejected by those of higher birth into whose ranks he had been intruded through the king's actions rather than his own. But it should be remembered that, in periods of civil strife, false accusations of slander were not uncommon: in the middle years of Edward II's reign, several people were brought before the king's council in the exchequer, accused, wrongly in some cases, of uttering 'unseemly words' (*verba indecencia*) against the king himself.[4] More interesting is the charge that Gaveston had one retainer of the earl of Lancaster ejected from office to make room for one of his own

---

[1] *Vita*, p. 8.   [2] Ibid., p. 25.   [3] Tout, *Place of Edw. II*, p. 12 n. 2.
[4] T. Madox, *The History and Antiquities of the Exchequer* . . . , 2nd edn., ii (London, 1769), 84–5; Conway Davies, *Baron. Opp.*, pp. 243, 271, 329, 553 (no. 19); Hilda Johnstone, 'The Eccentricities of Edward II', *EHR* 48 (1933), 266–7.

retainers.[5] It has been suggested that this might be a reference to the appointment, about Michaelmas 1311, of Arnaud de Tilh as marshal of the exchequer, a post which, at the time, it was the privilege of Nicholas de Segrave, a retainer of the earl of Lancaster, to fill in his capacity as marshal of England. Arnaud had been appointed by the king after the dismissal of Jocelin de Brankescombe, whose appointment, although also made by the king a year earlier, had been accepted by Segrave.[6] Whether Arnaud owed his appointment to Gaveston is uncertain, but it is made likely by the fact that both he and his father Bourgeois de Tilh were included in the list of those who according to the Ordinances were to be removed from the king's entourage, and that they originated from Tilh in the Landes (*arrondissement* of Dax, *canton* of Pouillon), less than 40 miles as the crow flies from Gabaston, the seat of Gaveston's family in Béarn.[7] It may be objected, however, that Jocelin de Brankescombe, the dismissed marshal of the exchequer, was neither a retainer of the earl of Lancaster nor even the original nominee of Nicholas de Segrave. We may also wonder why, if it is to the office of marshal of the exchequer that the *Vita* refers, it should place the incident immediately after the return of Gaveston from his Irish exile in June 1309, two years before the dismissal of Brankescombe and his replacement by Arnaud de Tilh.

Perhaps what the author of the *Vita* had in mind was the famous dispute concerning the succession to the lordship of Powys in Wales between Griffin de la Pole, a retainer of the earl of Lancaster, and Hawys, wife of John Charlton, Gaveston's retainer and *secretarius*.[8] The dispute, of course, was not, strictly speaking, about an 'office', but about land and power. It was most unfortunate for Gaveston that it should have arisen just at the time of his return from Ireland and that one of the parties should have been someone as close to him as Charlton. After the death of the lord of Powys in June 1309, an inquisition *post mortem* was held and Hawys declared the heir, following which, on 9 August, a privy seal writ ordered the escheator to deliver seisin of the lands to Hawys and her husband John

---

[5] *Vita*, p. 8.   [6] Maddicott, *Lancaster*, pp. 117–18; Hamilton, *Gaveston*, p. 89.
[7] *Gaveston's Jewels*, p. 17; *Gascon Rolls*, iv, ed. Y. Renouard, no. 852 n., and p. 641.
[8] On this dispute, see Conway Davies, *Baron. Opp.*, pp. 130 and n. 3, 212–13, 216–17; Maddicott, *Lancaster*, pp. 140–1.

Charlton.[9] Griffin, claiming that he was the legitimate heir according to Welsh laws and customs, soon resorted to force, which led to the seizure of his lands into the king's hands. The earl of Lancaster espoused his cause and, through him, the Powys dispute became an important issue in the negotiations of 1312–13 for the settlement of the question of the 'Newcastle jewels'.[10] There may have been another, incidental, consequence of the dispute: if Lancaster imagined that Gaveston had been directly involved in it on Charlton's side and had thus had a hand in the infringement of the Welsh laws of inheritance, he might have thought it particularly appropriate, when the time came for Gaveston's execution in Blacklow, that the executioners should be two Welshmen,[11] who were perhaps selected from the 'wild and fierce horde of Welshmen' in the retinue of the earl of Hereford.[12]

The charge regarding the removal of royal officials by Gaveston and their replacement by some of his followers also occurs in the Ordinances of 1311, which add that the officials removed were 'good ministers', whereas the aliens and others who were put in their place broke the law at Gaveston's command. The Ordinances also blamed Gaveston for giving evil counsel to the king, taking possession of all the royal treasure, and sending it abroad, accroaching royal power and purchasing out of the king's treasure alliances against all men, acquiring crown lands for himself and procuring grants of the same for others, having blank charters sealed with the great seal, and obtaining pardons for thieves and murderers; all this had been done treasonably, to the great damage of the king and disinheritance of the crown.[13]

Some of the accusations had already been made in the articles of 1308,[14] but the indictment of 1311 was much longer. Whether all the

---

[9] Conway Davies, *Baron. Opp.*, p. 217.   [10] *Gaveston's Jewels*, pp. 7–10, 12, 16, 20.
[11] *Vita*, p. 27.
[12] Ibid., p. 32. That the earl of Hereford was closely involved in Gaveston's murder is suggested by the letters in which the earls of Lancaster and Warwick promised, on 18 June 1312, the eve of the murder, 'to live and die in aid and defence of the said earl in the quarrel aforesaid'; earlier in the letters, the 'quarrel' was described as 'touching Sir Piers Gaveston' (Conway Davies, *Baron. Opp.*, p. 598; Maddicott, *Lancaster*, pp. 128–9; Phillips, *Pembroke*, p. 35). If every baronial leader, however, issued similar letters for each of the others (Maddicott, *Lancaster*, p. 128 n. 7), which I doubt, the argument would be of no value.
[13] *Rot. Parl.* i. 283; *Statutes*, i. 162; *BIHR* 57 (1984), 201–2.
[14] Richardson and Sayles, *The Governance of Mediaeval England*, p. 468; *Bridlington*, p. 34.

charges were deserved may well be questioned, but it certainly was true that Gaveston's friendship with the king had brought him and his followers territorial and financial gains, not to mention offices.[15] As late as February 1311 the king had sent from Berwick-upon-Tweed his favourite clerk of the wardrobe and privy seal Thomas de Newhay to the chancery in London to take charge there of the writing of seven charters of free warren in Gaveston's favour, see to their sealing with the great seal, and bring them back to Gaveston in Berwick. The clerk's expenses for this mission are summarized as follows in the wardrobe book of the king's fourth regnal year:

To Thomas de Nova Haya, clerk, sent by the king from Berwick-upon-Tweed to the chancery in London for writing seven charters granting [free] warren to the earl of Cornwall in several of his manors within the kingdom of England, and for sealing them with the king's great seal in the aforesaid chancery, and for taking them safely to the said earl from London to Berwick, for money paid by him for the green wax, silk laces, and parchment bought by him for the charters aforesaid, for seven leather boxes bound with iron also bought by him to put them in, for 6 ells of waxed hemp, for the wages of one clerk who helped him with the aforesaid charters, for one wicker chest in which to place the writs proclaiming the said charters, as well as for his expenses from 10 February in the present year, on which day he left the court in Berwick, until 13 June, both days included, for 124 days which he spent attending to the aforesaid business, except thirty-five days which he spent on his own affairs, receiving each day 12d., because he was off the marshal's roll during the same period, as appears in the particulars of his account, which he delivered into the wardrobe in London on 21 March in the sixth year, 115s. 5d.[16]

---

[15] Conway Davies, *Baron. Opp.*, pp. 83–4; Maddicott, *Lancaster*, pp. 79, 118; Hamilton, *Gaveston*, pp. 44, 75–6.

[16] BL MS Cotton Nero C viii, fo. 25ʳ: 'Thome de Nova Haya, clerico, misso per regem de Ber' super Twedam usque London' ad cancellariam pro vij cartis (de garenna [*interlined*]) domini comitis Cornubie [*de Garenna struck out*] ad diversa maneria sua infra regnum Anglie habenda scribendis et in cancellaria predicta sub magno sigillo ipsius regis consignandis et pro eisdem de London' usque Ber' ad dictum comitem salvo et secure deferendis, pro denariis per ipsum solutis tam pro cera viridi, laqueis de serico, pargameno emptis per ipsum pro cartis predictis, vij cophinis de corio ferro ligatis emptis similiter per ipsum pro eisdem imponendis, vj ulnis de canabi cereato, stipendiis unius clerici coadjuvantis circa cartas predictas, uno hanaperio de virgis empto pro brevibus de proclamacione cartarum predictarum imponendis, quam pro expensis suis a xᵒ die februarii, anno presenti [*quarto struck out*], quo die recessit de curia apud Berewicum, usque xiij diem junii, utroque computato, per cxxiiij dies, per quos fuit intendens negocio predicto, exceptis xxxv diebus per quos fuit in negociis suis propriis, percipienti per diem xij d., quia extra rotulum marescalli per idem tempus, sicut patet per particulas suas in garderoba per ipsum liberatas London' xxj die marcii, anno sexto, cxv s. v d.'

The intrusion of a wardrobe and privy seal clerk into the chancery
was highly irregular, but Thomas de Newhay was not new to such
irregularities: it will be remembered that it was he, and not a
chancery clerk, who had written the first document of the reign to be
sealed with the great seal, namely the charter of 6 August 1307 which
granted the earldom of Cornwall to Gaveston.[17]

One of those who benefited from their close connections with
Gaveston was Arnaud Guillaume de Marsan, one of his brothers. By
royal letters patent under the great seal dated 27 June 1308, he had
been appointed seneschal of Agenais,[18] an appointment which,
according to ordinances enacted at Condom in 1289 while Edward I
was in the duchy of Guyenne, should not have been made by the king
under the great seal, but by his representative in the duchy, the
seneschal of Gascony, under his seal of office, the seal of the Court of
Gascony.[19] In late November of the same year, another royal grant,
made jointly to Arnaud Guillaume and to Piers (who by then was in
Ireland), gave them castles, lands, and revenues in various parts of
the duchy of Guyenne.[20] The powerful Amanieu d'Albret objected to
these grants and tried to have them revoked by Edward II on the
ground that they were prejudicial to him, Edward, as king-duke, to
his honour, and to the interests of his kingdom, and that they had
been made to unworthy men. Having failed in his approach to
Edward and fearing that he might be subjected to unjust acts of
oppression by Arnaud Guillaume, his enemy, who had boasted that
he would take away from him the town of Nérac (*département* of Lot-et-
Garonne), Amanieu appealed to the king of France in January
1310.[21] It was probably in response to Amanieu's appeal that, later
on in the year, in order to forestall difficulties with France, Arnaud
Guillaume de Marsan was removed from his office as seneschal of
Agenais by his superior, John de Hastings, seneschal of Gascony and
of the duchy as a whole. In the autumn, soon after the arrival of the
earl of Richmond (Gaveston's friend) and of the other commissioners
sent to Gascony to reform its administration, the matter came up

[17] See above, ch. 2.
[18] *Gascon Rolls,* iv, ed. Renouard, no. 110 and p. xxvi.
[19] Chaplais, *EMDA* VIII. 66–8; J.-P. Trabut-Cussac, 'Actes gascons dispersés . . .', *Bulletin philologique et historique, Année 1962,* 1965, p. 126 (XIV).
[20] *Gascon Rolls,* iv, ed. Renouard, nos. 154–5, 157–8.
[21] Pau, Archives départementales des Pyrénées-Atlantiques, E 20.

before them and on 11 December 1310 it was decided that, in spite of Amanieu d'Albret's complaints, Arnaud Guillaume should be reinstated as seneschal of Agenais. Accordingly, John de Hastings reinvested him with that office by handing his glove to him ('per cirotecam suam'), but by then Arnaud Guillaume had had enough; he resigned the office immediately into the hands of Richmond, saying that he had no craving for offices ('dicens se non esse cupidum ballivarum').[22]

The punishment decreed in the Ordinances of 1311 for Gaveston's alleged offences was perpetual exile as in 1308, but it was to be applied more severely. Gaveston was to leave from the port of Dover and from nowhere else by 1 November 1311. He could take refuge in none of the king's lands on this side of the sea or beyond, which meant that England, Wales, Ireland, Gascony, and even Ponthieu were forbidden lands. If he remained anywhere in the king's lordship after the appointed date, he would be treated as the enemy of the king and of his people, and whoever infringed the decree of exile would, if convicted, be punished accordingly.[23] Anyone who contravened the Ordinances in general was also excommunicated *ipso facto*.[24]

The *Annales Londonienses* state that Gaveston did not leave the country by the appointed date, but two days later, on 3 November 1311 ('in triduo post festum Omnium Sanctorum') and that, instead of sailing from Dover, as decreed by the Ordinances, he boarded a ship on the Thames and landed *inter Rutenos*, at a place which has so far defied identification, but can only have been somewhere along the coast of northern France or Flanders.[25] The king's original intention, it seems, was that Gaveston should spend at least part of his exile in Brabant and make his way there through France. On 9 October Edward wrote to the duke of Brabant and his lieutenant as well as to the duchess, his own sister, asking them to receive Gaveston (described as 'nobilem virum dominum Petrum de Gavaston' comitem Cornubie') with kindness, to order the duke's subjects to treat him honourably

---

[22] *Gascon Rolls*, iv, ed. Renouard, p. xxvi and n. 2. For other examples of a glove being handed over as a symbol of investiture, see *La Chanson de Roland*, ed. F. Whitehead (Oxford, 1968), lines 247, 268, 320, 341, etc.; M. H. Keen, *The Laws of War in the Late Middle Ages* (London, 1965), p. 166.

[23] Kathleen Edwards in *EHR* 59 (1944), 321.

[24] Ibid.

[25] *Ann. Lond.*, p. 202.

while he stayed in the duchy, and to send a prompt reply.[26] Next day, royal letters of credence addressed to Philip IV were issued on behalf of Gerard Salveyn, knight, and Master Edmund of London, clerk, or either of them; in this case, too, Edward indicated that a prompt reply would be appreciated.[27] Salveyn's mission to France, which lasted from 13 October to 23 November, was to obtain a safe-conduct for Gaveston ('ad dominum regem Francie ad conductum pro domino Petro de Gavaston' comite Cornubie de eodem querendum').[28] How the king of France and the duke of Brabant responded to Edward's requests is not known, but, unless the safe-conduct proved difficult to obtain, Salveyn had enough time to return to England with it by early November, escort Gaveston to a safe place on the Continent, and be back at the royal court in London by 23 November. The story is slightly complicated by a tantalizing reference, in the household accounts of Queen Isabella, to a payment made to the messenger William Bale on 29 October, just a few days before Gaveston sailed, for delivering a letter from the queen to the receiver of Ponthieu 'concerning the affairs of the earl of Cornwall' (*pro negociis comitis Cornubie*);[29] this does not necessarily mean that Gaveston was to spend any length of time in Ponthieu, but it suggests that, willingly or unwillingly, the queen had agreed to help Gaveston in his plight, at least financially; from the way in which Gaveston is referred to as 'the earl of Cornwall' we may be entitled to presume sympathy for him, rather than hostility, from the queen's entourage and possibly from the queen herself. In the first half of October, Blasius of Siena, a Frescobaldi merchant, had been sent by Gaveston himself to Brabant and 'elsewhere', presumably to make further financial arrangements on his behalf. Blasius was back in Windsor Park by 19 October, on

---

[26] *Foedera*: R. II. i. 144. The great seal was in the king's hands from 28 Sept. 1311 (the day after the publication of the Ordinances in St Paul's churchyard) until 9 Dec., when it was returned to its [baronial] keepers (Conway Davies, *Baron. Opp.*, p. 127 and n. 6; Tout, *Chapters*, vi. 7; *Parl. Writs*, II. ii, app. pp. 42–4; *CCR 1307–1313*, pp. 438, 443). During that period, in which the chancellor Walter Reynolds, the king's creature, was in charge of the sealing, references to Gaveston give him the title of earl of Cornwall, for example in the letters of protection and attorney granted to him on 22 Oct. for five years (*CPR 1307–1313*, p. 397); for an apparent exception, see below, n. 34.

[27] *Foedera*: R. II. i. 145; *Treaty Rolls*, i, ed. Pierre Chaplais, no. 499.

[28] BL MS Cotton Nero C viii, fo. 65ʳ, where Salveyn's expenses are recorded 'a xiijᵒ die octobris, quo die iter arripuit versus Paris' ad regem predictum, usque xxiij diem novembris, quo die rediit ad curiam London', utroque computato, per xlij dies'; *Treaty Rolls*, i. 199 n. 2.

[29] *Isabella's Household Book*, p. 208.

which day the king gave him 6 marks as a compensation for the loss of a horse, which had died in Dover during the mission.[30]

The birth of Joan and Gaveston's fatal return

According to the *Annales Paulini*, Gaveston spent his exile in Flanders, staying in Bruges until after Christmas ('usque post festum Natalis Domini proximum sequens'), and then returned to England, where he was once again reinstated by the king. In the next paragraph, however, the annalist contradicts himself:

In the same year the king spent the feast of the Nativity in York and the aforesaid Piers was with him, and they stayed there until the following Easter.[31]

Not only was it impossible for Gaveston to have stayed in Bruges until after Christmas and to have celebrated the same feast with the king in York, but in any case Edward was in Westminster at Christmas 1311, not in York.[32] The author of the *Vita* also makes the two adoptive brothers spend Christmas together in York, but, unlike the annalist of St Paul's, he is consistent. According to him, Gaveston had returned well before Christmas; he had been moving around cautiously and it was thought that he had been hiding now in the king's chamber, now in Wallingford, now in the castle of Tintagel.[33] This was in fact nothing more than another version of the wild rumour which had led to a useless man-hunt in the south-west as early as 30 November. A great seal writ dated on that day—obviously at the command of the baronial council without the king's approval—ordered Hugh

[30] BL MS Cotton Nero C viii, fo. 83ᵛ.

[31] *Ann. Paul.*, p. 271: 'Eodem anno rex tenuit Nathalem apud Eboracum, et predictus dominus Petrus cum eo: et ibi morabantur usque Pascha proximum sequens.'

[32] Hallam, *Itinerary*, p. 80; Maddicott, *Lancaster*, pp. 121–2. As pointed out by Hamilton (*Gaveston*, p. 93), a messenger of Gaveston (Walter Dymmok) received on 23 Dec. at Westminster 20s. from the wardrobe for the expenses he was about to incur returning to his master with a royal reply to a letter which he had brought from him; see BL MS Cotton Nero C viii, fo. 84ʳ: 'Dymmok' nuncio comitis Cornubie, venienti ad regem cum litteris dicti comitis et redeunti ad eundem cum litteris regis, de dono ipsius regis nomine expensarum suarum sic redeundo, per manus proprias ibidem [sc. apud Westm'] xxiij die decembris, nunciante domino Willelmo de Melton' ex parte regis, xx s.' Such a substantial gift 'by way of expenses' to a mere messenger suggests that the distance which he would have to cover to rejoin Gaveston was a fairly long one; this makes it likely that Gaveston was still out of England at the time.

[33] *Vita*, p. 21.

Courtenay and William Martin to search every castle and fortress in Cornwall, Devon, Somerset, and Dorset, and every other place where they thought that they might find Gaveston. But the writ did not suggest that Gaveston had returned from exile; it stated that there were rumours that, instead of leaving the country as the Ordinances prescribed, he was still hiding ('adhuc latitat') and moving from place to place. In other words, it was believed that he had never left the country at all.[34] At the time of the writ, however, Gaveston was so far from hiding anywhere in England that a request for an extension of his safe-conduct—perhaps due to expire at Christmas—was about to be made to Philip the Fair. The envoy chosen for the mission was again Gerard Salveyn, who, having come back from his earlier visit to the Continent on 23 November, left for France a week later, on 1 December ('ad conductum . . . per longius tempus quam quod prius quesivit duraturum querendum'), to return to the king at Knaresborough on 13 January 1312; on this second mission, Salveyn's clerical companion was Master John de Percy.[35]

The first mission of Salveyn had lasted forty-two days and his second forty-four, in both cases an uncommonly long time for an uncomplicated errand. It has been suggested above that, on the first occasion, Salveyn had escorted Gaveston to his place of exile; perhaps on the second he escorted Gaveston back to England. If so, Gaveston arrived with him in Knaresborough, where the king was, on Thursday, 13 January. This is in fact practically confirmed by a draft news-letter, which is undated but was certainly written in January 1312. The relevant passage of the letter, which names neither its sender nor its addressee, but was possibly meant for the archbishop of York, states that 'this Thursday' the king arrived in York with the bishop of Chester (Walter Langton), the earl of Cornwall, and others:

---

[34] *Foedera*: R. II. i. 151; Maddicott, *Lancaster*, pp. 121–2. Compare *Vita*, p. 34. Because the great seal was in the king's hands on 30 Nov., not to be returned to its baronial keepers until 9 Dec. (above, n. 26), the writ was perhaps not presented to the seal until after the latter date; but if it was, the king and his close associates, including Reynolds, the chancellor, had no reason to object to its sealing and delay the dispatch of Courtenay and Martin on a wild-goose chase.

[35] BL MS Cotton Nero C viii, fo. 65ʳ, where Salveyn's expenses are recorded 'a primo die decembris, quo die recessit versus partes predictas, usque xiij diem januarii, quo die rediit ad regem usque Knaresburgh', utroque die computato, per xliiij dies'; *Treaty Rolls*, i. 199 n. 2; PRO E 101/373/26, fo. 45ᵛ; E 403/157, m. 1.

We let you know, my lord, that the king came to York this Thursday; he is staying at the palace and your houses have been taken for the earl's use. The bishop of Chester, the earl of Cornwall, Sir Henry de Beaumond, and Sir Ralph fitz William came with the king, and he has decided to stay there until Easter.[36]

Since the king is known to have been in Knaresborough, only 18 miles from York, on Thursday, 13 January and in York on Tuesday 18th,[37] the Thursday on which, according to the letter, he and Gaveston came to York can only have been that very Thursday 13th. In other words, as soon as Gaveston arrived in Knaresborough with Salveyn, the king and he and a few others rushed on their way to York.

The reason for the hasty journey was not a political crisis, but an important family event in Gaveston's life, the birth of his one and only daughter Joan: 'Not long after Epiphany (6 January)', wrote the canon of Bridlington (in Yorkshire), 'he [sc. Gaveston] arrived, in the king's company, in York, where the countess, his wife, gave birth to a daughter, for which reason he stayed there for some time'.[38] Although the canon, like the author of the *Vita*, wrongly makes Gaveston return to England before Christmas, he gets the 'local events' of importance right, the birth of Joan and the arrival of the king and Gaveston in York. He does not give the precise date of the birth, but we can probably work it out. Another interesting text tells us that King Robert and other minstrels, who entertained the king and magnates in the houses of the Friars Minor in York on the day on which the countess of Cornwall was churched, received 40 marks of the king's gift on 20 February 1312.[39] If the gift was made on the actual day of the churching of Margaret de Clare, as is likely, and if the churching took place forty days after confinement, as was usual, Joan would

---

[36] PRO SC 1/xxxvii/218 (Maddicott, *Lancaster*, p. 122, where the most important part of the letter is translated): 'Sachetz, sire, que le roi vint a Everwyk' ycest jeodi et gist au paleis, et vos maisons sount pris al eops le counte. Levesque de Cestre, le counte de Cornwaille, sire Henri de Beaumond et sire Rauf' le fuitz Williame vindrent ovesque le roy et il ad ordinez sa demere illeoques tauntque a la Pasque.'

[37] BL MS Cotton Nero C viii, fo. 65ʳ; *Foedera*: R. II. i . 153. The royal court and household, and the privy seal were in York from 13 Jan. to 24 Feb. inclusive (Hallam, *Itinerary*, p. 81).

[38] *Bridlington*, p. 42.

[39] BL MS Cotton Nero C viii, fo. 84ᵛ (cited by Hamilton, *Gaveston*, p. 94): 'Regi Roberto et aliis menestrallis diversis facientibus menestralcias suas coram rege et aliis magnatibus in domibus fratrum minorum Ebor' existentibus die purificacionis domine Margarete, comitisse Cornubie, de dono ipsius regis, per manus dicti regis Roberti recipientis denarios ad participandum inter eosdem apud Ebor' xx die februarii, xl mar.'

have been born on 12 January, the eve of Gaveston's arrival in Knaresborough. Hence the hurried journey to York.

Gaveston's daughter was born so soon after Christmas that it is easy to understand how, in a period in which rumours were rife and hard facts difficult to obtain, the festivities which followed the birth of Joan and her mother's churching may in one story have been confused with those associated with the Nativity of Christ. The contradiction in the *Annales Paulini* can now be explained; so can the error which the Annals share with the *Vita* regarding the presence of the king and Gaveston in York at Christmas 1311. They did not celebrate Christmas together in 1311 either in York or anywhere else, but they did share the celebrations of Joan's birth in that city. Since Gaveston was in Knaresborough on 13 January, he obviously had landed in England, presumably somewhere in the south, several days before his daughter's birth on the 12th, but not before Christmas. On this last point the confusion was made more likely by the rumour current in late November that Gaveston was then lurking in the south-west.

The birth of Joan also explains why Gaveston came back after just over two months in exile. Whether he was recalled or not is immaterial. He returned because he had learnt either in writing from the king or orally from Gerard Salveyn that the birth of his child was imminent. His return is unlikely to have been a defiance to the Ordainers. He understandably wished to be in England when his child was born and for the privilege he was prepared to risk his life, knowing that to the Ordainers and to all those who hated him he was still 'the enemy of the king and of his people', and a traitor; he must have been aware that, if he was captured, he almost certainly would be put to death. We have no means of telling whether his original intention had been to return into exile once the festivities were over. Had he tried to get back to the Continent and succeeded in doing so unharmed, he would no doubt have attracted a great deal of sympathy. But the king had decided for him that he should stay. Having once again the great seal under his control, Edward issued writs close under it on 18 January 1312, claiming that the exile against the earl of Cornwall had been decreed in defiance of the laws and customs of the realm, which in his coronation oath he had sworn to obverve. The sentence of exile had called the earl 'other than good and loyal' (a reference to the Ordinances, which declared him 'the enemy of the king and of his people'). As the earl was prepared to answer before the king any charge against him, Edward held him, as he had always done, 'bon et leal et a nostre fei et a nostre pees'. All the English sheriffs were ordered to publish the writs throughout their respective counties. Two days later, on 20 January, the sheriffs of all the counties in which the earl of Cornwall had held lands until they were seized into the king's hands as a result of his exile were ordered, also by writs under the great seal, to restore those lands to him.[40]

The writs of 18 and 20 January were a natural sequel to the king's announcement, made earlier in the month, that he had revoked the Ordinances as a whole. On the Sunday before or after he arrived in York (9 or 16 January), Edward had told an assembly of 'knights and other good people of the county of York' that what he had done and granted in London (that is to say, his confirmation of the Ordinances) had been done against his will, and that he had now repealed everything which the earls had ordained.[41] Since on Sunday 9th the king was in Knaresborough and on Sunday 16th in York, the latter date might be preferred on the ground that it would have been more appropriate for the leading men of Yorkshire to be summoned to a meeting in York, the capital city of their county, than in Knaresborough. It may be argued, however, that the earlier Sunday makes better sense, because it was on that day, 9 January, that a privy seal writ was issued which ordered the mayor of London not to allow anyone to enter the city 'with any kind of force' either to hold deliberations or for

[40] *Foedera*: R. II. i. 153–4. According to the *Annales Paulini* (p. 271), the writ of 18 Jan. was proclaimed in the Guildhall in London on Saturday 29th. A memorandum on the Close Roll claims that the writ had been drafted by the king himself, who handed all its exemplars as well as the great seal to the chancery spigurnel for sealing on the day and at the place mentioned in the writ, that is to say on 18 Jan. at York (*Foedera*: R. II. i. 153). This, however, does not seem to be strictly true. Another memorandum on the same Close Roll states that the three chancery clerks Adam Osgodby, Robert de Bardelby, and William Airmyn brought the great seal to the king in York on Tuesday in the feast of SS. Fabian and Sebastian ('die martis in festo'), and that next day the king had produced the seal still enclosed under the seals of the three clerks. In 1312 the feast of the two saints (20 Jan.) fell on a Thursday, not on a Tuesday. It looks therefore as if the words *die martis in festo* should be corrected to *die martis ante festum*, i.e. Tuesday, 18 Jan. It follows that the sealing of the writ could not have taken place until Wednesday, 19 Jan. (*Parl. Writs*, II. ii, app. pp. 43–4).

[41] PRO SC 1/xxxvii/218 (Maddicott, *Lancaster*, pp. 122–3; see n. 36, above): '. . . Sire, a cest dymaigne avoyt le roy devaunt luy chivalers et autres bones gentz du count[e] Deverwyk' et lur dyst que quantquil fist et granta a Loundres fust cuntre sa volunt[e], et totes le[s] choses que les countes ount fait et ordinez si ad il repelez, et les ad priez queux li aident de luy maintenir en son droyt, et il les meintendra countre touz autres'.

any other purpose.[42] The king could not fail to expect the earls to be so incensed by the news of his revocation of the Ordinances that they would wish to meet, preferably in London, and discuss their next move. Elementary wisdom therefore dictated that a royal order forbidding such meetings should reach London no later than the revocation notice.

The king did not have to wait long for the response of the earls. It is highly probable that the letter which he received from the earl of Lancaster shortly before 30 January was connected with the repeal of the Ordinances and with the return of Gaveston.[43] Perhaps it was the letter of credence or procuration of the solemn envoys who, according to Trokelowe, were sent to Edward by Lancaster in his capacity as elected leader of the community of the realm.[44] The envoys' mission, which, if we believe Trokelowe, was to beg the king either to hand over Gaveston to them or to send him back into exile,[45] was unlikely to achieve its objective, but Edward made a slight effort at conciliation by toning down, although only marginally, the measures which he had decreed on 9 January in Knaresborough. In the first place, not only did he no longer insist on the complete repeal of the Ordinances, but, by great seal writs dated 26 January, he ordered all the sheriffs in England to proclaim that the Ordinances were to be enforced as long as they were neither to his prejudice or that of the crown, nor contrary to the established laws and customs of the realm.[46] In the second place, a privy seal writ of 31 January, addressed to the mayor and aldermen of the city of London, specifically excepted the earls and barons from the prohibition to enter the city; they were to be allowed in to carry on their business, provided that they had neither horses nor arms, and that 'there was no suspicion of evil'.[47]

The earls and barons must have soon realized that the king's apparent concessions did not amount to much. In so far as 'the enemy of the king and of his people' was concerned, Edward had not moved one inch. The statement in the great seal writs of 18 and 20 January that Gaveston had been exiled against the laws and customs of the realm had not been recanted. Therefore the section of the Ordinances

[42] Parl. Writs, II. ii, app. p. 44.
[43] Maddicott, Lancaster, p. 124.
[44] Trokelowe, p. 74.   [45] Ibid.
[46] Foedera: R. II. i. 154.
[47] Parl. Writs, II. ii, app. p. 46.

which dealt with Gaveston's exile was one of those which the later writs of 26 January reserved as exempt from the enforcement order. Our knowledge of what happened next we owe to one single source, the Annals of London, which state that, when it dawned upon the magnates of the realm that they had been duped by the king, whose revocation of the Ordinances had brought all their work to naught, they went mad ('vehementi furore repleti'), and that, not long after the arrival from York of the privy seal writ of 31 January which allowed them to enter the city of London, they met in St Paul's together with the prelates to consider what they were to do.[48] At that meeting, which, although the annalist does not say so, took place in fact on 13 March, they resolved to capture Gaveston by throwing a vast circular net around the royal court. The country was divided into four zones, each of which was assigned to a separate keeper: the earl of Gloucester for Kent, Surrey, Sussex, and the south, including London; the earl of Lancaster for Wales and the west; the earl of Hereford for Essex and the east; and finally Robert de Clifford and Henry de Percy for the northern border. The annalist specifies that the task given to Clifford and Percy was to seal the northern border and prevent the king and Gaveston from holding talks with Robert Bruce and seeking his help. It is probable that the duties of each of the other keepers also consisted mainly of controlling access to his own zone. The only offensive operation in the plan was left to the earls of Pembroke and Warenne, who were to capture Gaveston and inform the king.[49]

We may wonder how the London annalist obtained his information on the earls' plan, the success of which, as rightly noted in the *Vita*, depended so much on complete secrecy.[50] The fact that it was at a meeting held in St Paul's that the plan was evolved and that our knowledge of it is based entirely on the account of an annalist, also from London, suggests a contemporary leak due to someone who attended the meeting. The culprit may have been Walter Langton, bishop of Coventry and Lichfield (alias of Chester), about whom Robert of Reading had some scathing remarks to make under the year 1311:

---

[48] *Ann. Lond.*, pp. 203–4; *Councils and Synods*, ed. F. M. Powicke and C. R. Cheney, II. ii (Oxford, 1964), 1371 n. 1; *Reg. Simonis de Gandavo*, i. 418–19.
[49] *Ann. Lond.*, pp. 203–4.   [50] *Vita*, p. 23; Maddicott, *Lancaster*, pp. 123–4.

Towards the end of the present year [that is to say, shortly before 25 March 1312], Walter Langton, bishop of Chester, forgetting that he owed his recent release from prison to the magnates of the land, did a complete about-turn and, imitating Achitofel to the great disgrace of his [episcopal] rank, sided with Piers Gaveston, to whom he did not hesitate to reveal the secret plans of the Ordainers.

Robert goes on to say that, as a result of his actions, Langton was, at a full council of the community of the realm, proclaimed a public traitor of the kingdom, and that finally, after several warnings, Archbishop Winchelsey excommunicated him at the provincial council of 8–14 May.[51] If Langton attended the meeting at St Paul's on 13 March when the plan for capturing Gaveston was decided on, we can be sure that he would have passed on the information to the king and Gaveston. By mid-January he was said to be the closest person to the king after Gaveston and by then Edward had already chosen him as treasurer.[52]

Whatever the source of the annalist's information may have been, two provisions in the plan make its authenticity highly probable. The first concerns the watch which was to be kept on the northern border; its purpose was not to guard against possible Scottish incursions, but to prevent the king and Gaveston from holding talks with Robert Bruce and asking for his help. This was a reasonable precaution for the Ordainers to take, if it was true, as stated in the *Vita*, that Edward had made an approach to Bruce, offering him the peaceful possession of the Scottish kingdom in return for giving Gaveston temporary shelter,[53] or if it was believed that such an approach was going to be made. Even more convincing is the provision for Gaveston's actual capture, which in the alleged plan was entrusted to the earls of Pembroke and Warenne, two of the three baronial leaders, the third one being Henry de Percy, who did actually besiege Gaveston in Scarborough and accept his surrender on 19 May.[54]

---

[51] *Flores*, iii. 148–9: 'Circa presentis anni revolutionem temporum Walterus de Langetone episcopus Cestrensis . . . Petro de Gavastone adherere et secreta consilii tutorum regni non formidabat revelare'. It has been assumed here that Robert of Reading used the normal Annunciation dating-style of the English Church, which makes the year begin on 25 Mar. See also *Councils and Synods*, ed. Powicke and Cheney, II. ii (Oxford, 1964), 1371–2 (XII).

[52] PRO SC 1/xxxvii/218 (Maddicott, *Lancaster*, p. 122; see n. 36, above): 'Levesque de Cestre ad touz ces terres delivres et est tresorer jurez, et est le plus prive du roy apres le counte'.

[53] *Vita*, p. 22.   [54] Ibid., p. 24; *Ann. Lond.*, p. 204.

Some time between 7 and 12 March, only a matter of days before the St Paul's meeting charged the earls of Gloucester, Lancaster, Hereford, Pembroke, and Warenne with the execution of the plan, Queen Isabella wrote from St Albans to each of the five earls. The contents of the letters are unknown, but, if they were connected with politics, it is probable that the queen, who was then in the second month of her pregnancy and about to join her husband in York, pleaded for peace and moderation.[55] But neither the king nor the earls were in a compromising mood. By the beginning of April, there was still no sign that Edward would ever be prepared to forsake his adoptive brother. Indeed Gaveston's reinstatement process, which had been set in motion on 18 January, was still in progress on 3 April, on which day a great seal letter restored him to the office of justice of the forest north of the Trent, which he had held from 1 October 1310 until the Ordinances.[56] This reappointment was a diplomatic blunder, not only because it contravened the Ordinances, but also because an influential baron, Henry de Percy, an adherent of the earl of Lancaster, had to be removed from office to make room for Gaveston. It was contrary to the Ordinances for two reasons: firstly because Gaveston, having been branded by the Ordainers as an 'enemy of the king and of his people', could not hold office; secondly because the two offices of justice (or keeper) of the forest north and south of the Trent were among those which could only be filled with the assent of the barons in parliament.[57] In addition, Gaveston's reinstatement of 3 April 1312 was no more straightforward than his original appointment of 1 October 1310, because on neither occasion was the office vacant: in October 1310 it was held for life by John de Segrave, a retainer of the earl of Lancaster,[58] and in April 1312 during pleasure by Henry de Percy, also an adherent of Lancaster and one of the two barons who were to be directly involved in the anti-Gaveston plan devised in St Paul's a fortnight earlier.[59] Both Segrave and Percy, were, it is true, given a pecuniary compensation by Gaveston for vacating their office, but it is difficult to believe that

---

[55] *Isabella's Household Book*, p. 138; Maddicott, *Lancaster*, p. 124.
[56] *Foedera:* R. II. i. 163; *CPR 1307–1313*, pp. 450–1; Conway Davies, *Baron. Opp.*, p. 487; Maddicott, *Lancaster*, p. 122.   [57] *Statutes*, i. 160 (XIV), 162 (XX).
[58] *CFR 1307–1319*, p. 73; *CPR 1307–1313*, pp. 450–1.
[59] *CFR 1307–1319*, p. 116; *CPR 1307–1313*, pp. 450–1.

either of them might, even for money, have resigned his post in Gaveston's favour of his own free will.[60]

Gaveston's reappointment as justice of the forest north of the Trent was, of course, consistent with the writ of 18 January which declared that he had been exiled against the laws and customs of the realm and therefore wrongly deprived of his lands, offices, and dignities;[61] it was also consistent with the writ of 26 January which ordered the enforcement of the Ordinances as long as they were neither prejudicial to the king and his crown nor contrary to the laws and customs of the realm.[62] But these were not arguments likely to find favour with the earls and barons, for whom the Ordinances had to be observed in their entirety, a point which they emphasized once again on 3 April, the date, as it happened, of Gaveston's reinstatement as justice of the forest north of the Trent.

Monday, 3 April 1312 was no ordinary date in the exchequer calendar; it was the morrow of the close of Easter (the eighth day after Easter Sunday) and, as such, the first day of the Easter term. In the morning of that day, Walter Langton, bishop of Chester, went to the Exchequer of Receipt in Westminster. Having gathered around him the barons, chamberlains, and other officials of the exchequer, he produced the great seal commission (of 23 January 1312) which appointed him as treasurer until next parliament,[63] and then he sat with them to receive the proffers of the sheriffs and bailiffs. The ceremony was about to be concluded when the earls of Pembroke and Hereford, John Botetourt, and others came in, saying through Botetourt's mouth that they had been sent by the archbishop (of Canterbury), the bishops, and other prelates, as well as by the earls, barons, and community of the realm. Then, after rehearsing how some ordinances on the state of the kingdom had been made, which the king had accepted and had had published, and which the prelates, earls, barons, and others had sworn to observe, Botetourt asked Langton whether he had taken the oath. When the bishop replied that he had, he was told bluntly by the same Botetourt, speaking on behalf of the community of the realm, that in that case he had committed

---

[60] Ibid.; Conway Davies, *Baron. Opp.*, p. 506, does not consider the possibility of coercion.

[61] *Foedera*: R. II. i. 153.   [62] Ibid. 154.

[63] For this commission, see *CPR 1307–1313*, p. 413; Conway Davies, *Baron. Opp.*, pp. 120, 389; Maddicott, *Lancaster*, p. 122.

perjury, since he was now acting as treasurer, although the Ordinances had prescribed that the holder of that office should be appointed with the assent of the barons in parliament.[64] He was therefore held as an adherent of the enemies of the realm. He was to stop meddling in the treasurer's office, if he did not wish worse things to happen to him. This was repeated by the earls of Pembroke and Hereford, who then told the chamberlains that, if they wished to keep themselves free from harm, they were not to deliver any money or any other treasure to 'anyone' through whom it could reach the enemy of the kingdom,[65] (that is to say, of course, Piers Gaveston).

Measures taken by the king at the beginning of April to strengthen the defences of Scarborough Castle are an indication that he had resigned himself to an armed confrontation with the earls and barons. Gaveston, who had been appointed keeper of the castle on 31 March, was ordered on 4 April, under pain of forfeiture, to surrender it to nobody but the king, and not even to him, should he be brought there as a prisoner; should the king die, the castle was to be kept by Gaveston for the king's heirs.[66] On 10 April Edward and Gaveston left York for Newcastle.[67] The reason for this move is mysterious. Why should the king at this juncture have wished to be closer to the Scottish border? According to a letter which he wrote to Philip the Fair on 1 April from York, he intended to take action against the Scots, who had recently crossed the border and were preparing to besiege Berwick-upon-Tweed.[68] Four days later, he issued writs ordering a large number of his Gascon vassals to get ready to come to him, when summoned, with a suitable retinue of men-at-arms, and to let him know meanwhile, in writing and through the bearer, how many men-at-arms they would bring with them. He was confident,

---

[64] As the letters patent of 23 Jan. 1312 appointed Langton as treasurer 'until next parliament', the king could argue that they did not infringe the Ordinances; it was only an interim appointment, which parliament, when it next met, could confirm or revoke.

[65] The whole story is told in a letter of the barons of the exchequer to the king; the letter is printed in Madox, *The History and Antiquities of the Exchequer* ..., 2nd edn., i (London, 1769), 267–8, note *o*, and in Conway Davies, *Baron. Opp.*, pp. 551–2; neither text is perfect. See also Tout, *Chapters*, ii. 234–5 n. 4.

[66] *CFR 1307–1319*, p. 129; *CPR 1307–1313*, p. 454; Maddicott, *Lancaster*, p. 124; Hamilton, *Gaveston*, pp. 94–5.

[67] *Bridlington*, p. 42: 'dominus rex non sano ductus consilio, regni regimen parvipendens, iiij^{to} idus Aprilis cum prefato Petro de Gavastone usque Novum Castrum super Tynam est profectus.'   [68] *Foedera*: R. II. i. 162.

the writs added, that they would help him, as they were bound to do by the faith and homage they owed him, to enhance his honour and royal dignity and ward off whatever wrongs might be done to him.[69]

It seems to be generally believed that Edward wanted the help of the Gascon feudal host to quell the English baronial rebellion which was expected to erupt at any moment. Assuming that he received a favourable response from his Gascon vassals, the troops which they might provide could not possibly arrive for several months, and they would run the risk of being decimated on landing. At least some of them might decline to come, on the ground that their privileges entitled them not to be summoned by Edward as their duke for any service outside the boundaries of their duchy.[70] One would have expected Gaveston and his Gascon friends in England to warn the king of that possibility. Perhaps Gascon help was required for possible military operations against the Scots, but the same objections would be raised in Gascony, and to envisage a campaign in Scotland when civil war threatened at home would have been sheer lunacy. Edward may, of course, have naïvely thought that his summons to his Gascon vassals might convince the English earls and barons that he did mean to go to war against Scotland, and that his move from York to Newcastle was the first step in that direction, whereas his real motive for getting nearer the Scottish border may have been to try to strike a bargain with Robert Bruce and offer him peace and stability in return for sheltering Gaveston.[71]

If the royal writs to the Gascons were just a ploy, the earl of Lancaster was not deceived, at least not for long. When the earl started his march towards Newcastle-upon-Tyne is not known, but he arrived there on 4 May with a strong force. He apparently took the city without encountering any real resistance, but Gaveston, the man he had come to capture, was no longer there. The king and he had only just left for Tynemouth, obviously in a great hurry, abandoning most of their valuables, including many jewels, and a large stock of arms as well as many horses, all of which were seized by Lancaster.[72]

For Gaveston, however, it was only a short reprieve. Before the middle of May, Scarborough Castle, where he had been left in charge

[69] Ibid. 163.
[70] For Edward's difficulties in obtaining Gascon help against the Scots in 1315–16, see *Gascon Rolls*, iv, ed. Renouard, pp. 568–74.   [71] *Vita*, p. 22.
[72] Maddicott, *Lancaster*, pp. 124–5; Hamilton, *Gaveston*, p. 95.

by the king, who had himself gone to Knaresborough, was besieged by the earls of Pembroke and Warenne and Henry de Percy. Gaveston surrendered on 19 May under certain conditions agreed between him and the besiegers, the latter acting on behalf of 'the community of the realm of England'.[73] The events of the next month, the last month of Gaveston's life, are too well known to need lengthy rehearsing, how Pembroke took sole charge of Gaveston, having perhaps been bribed to do so either by the king or by Gaveston himself, and how, on 10 June, Guy de Beauchamp, earl of Warwick, removed the latter forcibly from the rector's house in Deddington (Oxfordshire), where Pembroke had unwisely left him with inadequate protection, while he himself went to Bampton to see his wife. Beauchamp took his prisoner to Warwick Castle. There, after a meeting between the earls of Lancaster, Arundel, Hereford, and Warwick, and a mock trial, Gaveston was sentenced to death for treason. The sentence was carried out on 19 June in Blacklow, within the fee of the earl of Lancaster: one Welshman ran him through the body and another cut off his head.[74]

Why the earl of Warwick should have hated Gaveston so much that it made him in 1312 break all the accepted rules of chivalry is a mystery. It may have had something to do with Gaveston's marriage to Margaret de Clare. Warwick had once been betrothed ('per verba de futuro') to Isabella, daughter of Earl Gilbert of Gloucester (who died in 1295) by his first wife, Alice de la Marche. Margaret de Clare, who married Gaveston on 1 November 1307, was Gilbert's daughter by his second wife, Joan, daughter of Edward I. At the time of Gilbert's second marriage, Edward had imposed upon him a settlement which to all intents and purposes disinherited the children of the first marriage, including Isabella, to the benefit of the children to be born of the second marriage. Warwick's marriage to Isabella ('per verba de presenti') never took place, although a dispensation for it was obtained, at Edward I's request, from Boniface VIII in 1297, on the ground that the marriage would strengthen peace in the kingdom of England. As late as 1301, on account of dangers which might otherwise arise, efforts were still being made by Archbishop

[73] *Ann. Lond.*, p. 206; Maddicott, *Lancaster*, pp. 125–6; Hamilton, *Gaveston*, p. 96.
[74] *Vita*, pp. 25–7; *Ann. Lond.*, p. 207; Trokelowe, pp. 76–7; Maddicott, *Lancaster*, pp. 127–9; Phillips, *Pembroke*, pp. 35–6; Hamilton, *Gaveston*, pp. 97–9.

Winchelsey for the conclusion of the marriage by improving Isabella's financial prospects, but his efforts did not succeed. Gaveston's marriage to the wealthier Margaret de Clare may have made Warwick jealous.[75]

To the king, as expected, Gaveston's killing was murder, but to the earls it was a judicial act, the execution of an enemy of the king and of his realm and people.[76] They considered, John de Trokelowe tells us, that there could be no peace in the kingdom of England while Piers lived.[77] Although Trokelowe does not draw the parallel, Saul had said the same to Jonathan about David and the kingdom of Israel,[78] but, unlike Saul, the earls achieved their objective. During the negotiations for peace between the king and the earls which took place from the autumn of 1312 until the spring of 1313 through the mediation of the two papal envoys Arnaud d'Aux, bishop of Poitiers and later cardinal bishop of Albano, and Arnaud Novel, cardinal priest of S. Prisca, and of Philip IV's half-brother Louis, count of Evreux, the earl of Lancaster insisted, in his own name and in that of his adherents, that any guarantee from the king promising them immunity from prosecution for Gaveston's death should plainly state that what they had done 'about Gaveston' had been done because he was an enemy of the king and kingdom, and an outlaw. Had they done it for any other reason, the earl continued, they would have killed him unjustly and could not escape the charge of homicide.[79]

---

[75] See G. E. Cokayne, *Complete Peerage*, v. 707–8; xii. ii. 371; G. W. Watson, 'Alice de la Marche, countess of Gloucester and Hertford', *The Genealogist*, NS 38 (1922), 169–72; K. B. McFarlane, 'Had Edward I a "Policy" towards the Earls?', *History*, 50 (1965), 154; *Les Registres de Boniface VIII*, i, ed. A. Thomas, M. Faucon, and G. Digard (Bibliothèque des écoles françaises d'Athènes et de Rome, 1907), no. 1872; *Registrum Roberti Winchelsey, Cantuariensis archiepiscopi*, ed. Rose Graham, ii (Canterbury and York Society, lii, 1956), p. 741.

[76] *Gaveston's Jewels*, pp. 7, 16.

[77] Trokelowe, p. 69: 'vivente ipso Petro, pax in regno esse non poterit', p. 77; 'Ipso enim vivente, secura tranquillitas in terra Anglie esse non poterit.'

[78] 1 Sam. 20: 30–1.   [79] *Gaveston's Jewels*, p. 16.

5

THE NEWCASTLE JEWELS AND GAVESTON'S CHAMBERLAINSHIP

WHEN, as we have seen, the earl of Lancaster entered Newcastle-upon-Tyne on 4 May 1312, he found that the king and Gaveston had gone: having presumably received belatedly the news of the imminent arrival of Lancaster's army, the two adoptive brothers had fled to Tynemouth, leaving behind in Newcastle, with an inadequate guard, a considerable amount of jewels as well as arms and horses. Lancaster made the guards prisoner and took away the jewels, arms, and horses,[1] but according to the *Vita* it had never been his intention to treat these goods as booty: he had placed them in safe custody, so that what belonged to the king could be returned to him.[2] Later on, when the king accused Lancaster of having acted like an armed robber, the *Vita* makes the earl protest that he had done nothing of the kind: having found in Newcastle many goods which he knew to belong to the king lying there as derelict and therefore at the mercy of the occupant, he had taken action to save them for the king and he had them inventoried.[3] This portrayal of Lancaster as the selfless champion of the king's interests is not borne out by the surviving records of the negotiations of 1312–13 which led to the surrender of the jewels to the king. In their communications with the mediators, far from admitting that the goods captured in Newcastle were the king's, Lancaster and his adherents claimed that they were the goods of Gaveston, an enemy of the king and kingdom; it was as the escheated property of a felon that Lancaster was prepared to hand them over to

---

[1] Maddicott, *Lancaster*, p. 125.   [2] *Vita*, p. 23.   [3] Ibid., p. 35.

the king.[4] This argumentation was clearly designed to induce the king
to brand Gaveston as a traitor, which he had consistently refused to
do. Unlike Lancaster, the mediators were quite properly non-
committal: they spoke of 'the things which had been taken in
Newcastle and elsewhere by the occasion of Piers Gaveston, to
whomsoever they might belong', suggesting thereby the possibility of
more than one rightful owner.[5]

Lancaster's inventory: the jewels of the king and those of Gaveston

Lancaster's inventory of what he and his adherents called the goods of
Gaveston has survived, having been incorporated in the royal letters
of quittance which were issued on 27 February 1313, four days after
the overdue surrender of the goods to the king.[6] It shows beyond
doubt that the earl knew that at least those jewels which in the
inventory were noted as 'from the king's old treasure' (*du viel tresor le
roi*) had originally belonged to the king and had at some time been
stored in the royal wardrobe. In some cases, the compiler of the
inventory specified that he owed his information to the labels attached
to the items in question ('sicome piert par les billes'). Such were all
the staffs bearing diamonds, emeralds, rubies, sapphires, and other
precious stones, some of which were set in rings, received from the
executors of deceased bishops and abbots.[7] Some items in Lancaster's
inventory should therefore be traceable in earlier lists of wardrobe
jewels. Of the actual identifications which have so far been proposed
only four stand up to scrutiny,[8] but to these should be added at least
another seven, making it a total of eleven items about which we can be
reasonably certain that they came from the old store of the wardrobe.
The identified items are as follows:

1. a gold brooch with two emeralds, two rubies, four pearls, and a
sapphire in the centre; valued at 160 *livres tournois*;[9]

---

[4] *Gaveston's Jewels*, p. 7. [5] Ibid., pp. 3, 13, 18.
[6] *Foedera*: II. i. 203–5; below, App. II (the translation in Hamilton, *Gaveston*, pp. 119–27,
needs extensive corrections); Maddicott, *Lancaster*, p. 336.
[7] Below, App. II, items 40–56, 65.
[8] J. S. Hamilton, 'Piers Gaveston and the Royal Treasure', *Albion*, 23 (1991), 205–6. Of the
identifications proposed there, only items 1, 2, 4, and 5 can be accepted.
[9] Below, App. II, item 32; see *Liber Quot.*, p. 353.

2. a gold jewel with small emeralds, and with a black cameo in the centre, received from the bishop of Bath and Wells;[10]

3. in a pouch of cloth, several stones of various colours, which were received, by the hand of Hugh of Nottingham, from the bishop of Bath; from the old treasure; in the [twenty-]fifth year [of Edward I's reign];[11]

4. a gold ring with a sapphire, which St Dunstan made with his own hands;[12]

5. in a coffer bound with iron, an enamelled silver mirror, a comb, a pricket, given to the king [sc. Edward I] by the countess of Bar in Ghent;[13]

6. a pair of enamelled knives, given to the king [sc. Edward I] by the duchess of Brabant;[14]

7. another pair of enamelled knives;[15]

8. in another coffer, a silver belt with shields hooped with silver, enamelled, weighing four pounds ten shillings;[16]

9. a silver cup, which belonged to Archbishop Henry of York, weighing 46s. 8d., from the old treasure;[17]

10. in another coffer, in a casket, a purse embroidered with pearls, given by the countess of Flanders to the late king in Ghent;[18]

11. a purse of gold cloth with two stones from Jerusalem in it.[19]

By describing as Gaveston's goods the king's jewels which he had seized in Newcastle, Lancaster insinuated that the man he had had executed as a traitor in Blacklow had indeed misappropriated the royal treasure, as the Ordinances claimed. On the face of it, the evidence certainly seemed to point in that direction. The mere fact that some articles which belonged to the king were found in the same containers as others which were undoubtedly Gaveston's, for example horse housings bearing the royal arms and an old banner with the

[10] App. II, item 38; see Cole, *Documents*, p. 280.
[11] App. II, item 56; see *Liber Quot.*, p. 345; Cole, *Documents*, p. 281.
[12] App. II, item 57; see *Liber Quot.*, p. 348; Cole, *Documents*, p. 280.
[13] App. II, item 72; see *Liber Quot.*, p. 343; Cole, *Documents*, p. 280.
[14] App. II, item 73; see *Liber Quot.*, p. 344; Cole, *Documents*, p. 279.
[15] App. II, item 74; see *Liber Quot.*, p. 343; Cole, *Documents*, p. 279.
[16] App. II, item 77; see *Liber Quot.*, p. 349; Cole, *Documents*, p. 282.
[17] App. II, item 113; see Cole, *Documents*, p. 279.
[18] App. II, item 119; see *Liber Quot.*, p. 343.
[19] App. II, item 121; see *Liber Quot.*, p. 348; Cole, *Documents*, p. 280.

arms of Gaveston, might have been enough to convince the suspicious Lancaster that he had stumbled upon a hoard of what Gaveston was accused of having plundered from the king's treasury.[20]

In Lancaster's inventory we also find, interspersed among items which had without doubt belonged to the king, several jewels which are said to have been found on Gaveston's person when he was taken, including the most valuable item in the whole list, a large ruby *hors d'or* worth £1,000. Although it has been claimed that this was the gold ring with a large ruby, also valued at £1,000, formerly the property of Edmund, earl of Cornwall, which Edward I had given to his second wife, Queen Margaret,[21] this is very unlikely. Not only was Margaret still alive in 1312, but Edmund's large ruby, which she had acquired as the gift of Edward I, was set in a gold ring, whereas the ruby found on Gaveston was unset (*hors d'or*, the French equivalent of *sine auro*).[22] The only connections between the two jewels were that they had both been valued at £1,000 and that each of them had belonged to an earl of Cornwall. Whether Gaveston had acquired his ruby by purchase or as a gift, or in some other way, cannot be determined.

Gaveston's large ruby is followed in Lancaster's list by another ruby, called 'la cerise', set in a gold ring, which had belonged to the king. In turn, this royal ruby is followed by another item found on Gaveston's person when he was captured, namely an enamelled silver box containing three large rubies in rings as well as one emerald and one diamond of great value. Although 'la cerise' is not said to have been found on Gaveston, its place in the list, between two items which Gaveston had on him when he was taken, may have been deliberately chosen to suggest that it had been appropriated by Gaveston and, at the same time, that the unset ruby worth £1,000 and the contents of the silver box had also once belonged to the king. There seems no reason to doubt, however, that the jewels discovered on Gaveston's person were legitimately his own. Nor is there any evidence that *all* the jewels and other goods which had been abandoned in Newcastle

---

[20] App. II, items 173, 175.

[21] App. II, item 67; see Hamilton in *Albion*, 23 (1991), 206.

[22] BL MS Add. 7966 A, fo. 186 (parchment roll headed: 'Inventarium jocalium domine Margarete, regine Anglie, factum apud Turrim London' vj^to die junii, anno regni regis Edwardi xxx^mo . . .'): 'Anulus auri cum rubetto magno, quem rex dedit regine et qui fuit domini E[dmundi] quondam comitis Cornubie'. The jewels on Gaveston's person were probably seized by the earl of Warwick at Deddington rather than by the earl of Pembroke at Scarborough.

were regarded as Gaveston's property either by the king or by
Gaveston himself. In reality, the alleged Gaveston hoard was a mixed
collection of valuables, the majority of which still belonged to the
king, as it had always done, and most of the rest was Gaveston's.
Hasty packing, done perhaps at a time when it was hoped that goods
as well as persons could be evacuated from Newcastle, might easily
account for a certain amount of muddle: even two silver bowls
stamped with shields bearing the arms of Edmund de Mauley,
steward of the royal household, and presumably his own property,
were placed in the same coffer as a silver cup with the royal arms of
France and England, which we may assume to have formed part of
the royal treasure.[23] If the royal jewels seized by Lancaster had been
either misappropriated by Gaveston or given to him by the king, in
neither case would the labels which testified to their royal origin have
been left attached to them for anyone to read. Nor is it likely that
Edward would have considered parting with jewels of such senti-
mental value to him as the gold cup which his mother Eleanor of
Castile had bequeathed to him 'with her blessing'.[24] The gold ring
with a diamond, worth £10, which in October 1311, just before
leaving for his third and last exile, Gaveston is known to have been
given by the king, did not come from the old store of the wardrobe.
Like the pair of silver basins, worth 8 marks, which the king also gave
Gaveston in the same month, the ring had been bought by Ingelard de
Warle, keeper of the wardrobe, from the London goldsmith Roger de
Frowyk.[25] If Edward was in the habit of giving jewels from the royal
treasure to his adoptive brother, why did he not do so in October
1311 instead of resorting to special purchases? This is all the more
remarkable as, at the beginning of that month, he had a unique
opportunity for abstracting jewels from the wardrobe store without
attracting unwelcomed attention. Although the notorious burglary of
the wardrobe treasury at Westminster in April 1303 had demonstrated
that Westminster was not a safe repository,[26] a substantial collection
of royal jewels was still stored there as late as the autumn of 1311,
when it was at long last removed to the Tower of London. On 2
October, Henry del Neweheth, master of the royal barge called *la*

---

[23] App. II, items 176, 179.   [24] Ibid., item 87.
[25] BL MS Cotton Nero C viii, fo. 120ᵛ.   [26] See Tout, *Chapters*, ii. 55–8.

Swallow, who had been entrusted with the operation, received for himself and his fellows a gift of 10s. from the king. This is recorded in a wardrobe-book entry, which surprisingly escaped T. F. Tout's notice:

To Henry del Neweheth, master of the royal barge called la Swalwe, and to his fellows taking in a boat of the same ship from the treasury at Westminster to the Tower of London royal jewels which were in the said treasury, as a royal gift for their work, by their own hands there [sc. in London] on 2 October, 10s.[27]

That the removal of the jewels from Westminster to the Tower was done at the king's personal command can hardly be questioned. It happened, significantly, five days after the publication of the Ordinances in St Paul's churchyard (27 September) and nine days before they were sealed with the great seal (11 October).[28]

The royal jewels in Edward I's reign: their provenance and custody or disposal

At the time of Edward II's accession, the royal treasure represented a considerable fortune, worth much more than £100,000, the estimated value of the jewels *stricto sensu* and other precious objects which had been stolen from the wardrobe treasury at Westminster in 1303 and were for the most part recovered soon afterwards.[29] Some of these jewels Edward I had inherited with the throne, notably the coronation regalia and presumably such items as the gold ring which St Dunstan was supposed to have made with his own hands.[30] Others had been either forfeited to the king by their owners or purchased by the keeper of the wardrobe, as the jewel inventories in the wardrobe accounts of the reign show. In these inventories two other categories of valuable jewels are listed together under one heading, for example 'Jewels remaining at the end of the thirty-first year out of the jewels given to

[27] BL MS Cotton Nero C viii, fo. 82ᵛ: 'Henrico del Neweheth', magistro bargie regis que vocatur la Swalwe, et sociis suis ducentibus in quodam batello ejusdem navis de thesauraria Westm' usque Turrim London' jocalia regis in dicta thesau[ra]ria existencia, de dono regis pro labore suo, per manus proprias ibidem [sc. London'] secundo die octobris, x s.'

[28] Conway Davies, *Baron. Opp.*, pp. 366–7; Maddicott, *Lancaster*, p. 117.

[29] *Foedera*: R. I. ii. 959; Tout, *Chapters*, ii. 56.

[30] Below, App. II, item 57.

the king and returned to the king after the death of prelates in the thirtieth year'.[31] The first category consisted of precious objects of various kinds which had been presented to the king either by foreign rulers or by friends and relations. The second was made up of gold rings and silver cups which had belonged to dead bishops and abbots and had been delivered into the wardrobe by their executors; the delivery took place normally before the temporalities were restored to the dead prelate's successor and sometimes on the same day as the licence to elect a new bishop or abbot, or the assent to his election, had been obtained from the king.[32] As wealthy bishops and abbots owned a number of rings, it is impossible to say how often those brought into the wardrobe were the actual 'rings of office' which the bishops and abbots had worn while they were alive.[33] Edward I's wardrobe clerks, however, seem to have assumed that they always were, since they consistently refer to them as having been 'returned to the king' (regi restitutis), suggesting that in each case the ring had originally been given by the king to the bishop or abbot as a symbol of investiture, which in fact had not been the case for some 200 years. Why the silver cups were also said to have been returned to the king is more difficult to explain. Perhaps the rings and cups represented some kind of heriot, as has been suggested;[34] at any rate, their surrender into the wardrobe appears to have been no less obligatory than the payment of fines, euphemistically described as offerings ('oblata') in the early thirteenth century, for confirmations of charters of liberties and similar royal favours.

The day-book of the controller of the wardrobe for 1299–1300 also

---

[31] BL MS Add. 8835, fo. 123ʳ: 'Jocalia remanencia in fine anni xxxj de jocalibus regi datis et post decessum prelatorum regi restitutis anno xxxᵒ.'

[32] The ring of John le Romeyn, archbishop of York (died 11 Mar. 1296), was delivered into the wardrobe at Wark on 26 Mar. (Liber Quot., p. 345), the date of issue of the congé d'élire for his successor (CPR 1292–1301, p. 185); Henry Newark, the new archbishop, was elected on 7 May (Brit. Chron., p. 282). Thomas de Bitton, bishop of Exeter, having died on 21 Sept. 1307, the licence to elect his successor was issued on 6 Oct. and Walter de Stapeldon was elected on 13 Nov. The king gave his assent on 3 Dec., on which day Bitton's ring was brought to the wardrobe at Reading (Bodl. Lib. MS Tanner 197, fo. 62ʳ; John Le Neve, Fasti Ecclesiae Anglicanae, 1300–1541, ix (Exeter Diocese), comp. Joyce M. Horn (Athlone Press, London, 1964), p. 1).

[33] Walter de Merton, bishop of Rochester (1274–7), left on his death seven anuli preciosi worth 110s. and ten other rings worth 10s. (The Early Rolls of Merton College, Oxford, ed. J. R. L. Highfield (Oxford, 1964), pp. 92, 98, 101).

[34] Susan Wood, English Monasteries and their Patrons in the Thirteenth Century (Oxford Univ. Press, 1955), p. 88.

mentions Edward I's special or private jewels ('jocalia regis specialia' or 'privata'), which were stored separately in a small ivory chest ('scrinium eburneum') called 'forcerus cum jocalibus regis privatis', but, because the chest was locked and sealed with W[alter] Langton's seal, its contents could not be inventoried. The controller knew, however, that it contained rings, brooches, gems, purses, belts, and other small items of the same kind.[35]

While Edward I was hoarding such a wealth of precious objects in the coffers of the wardrobe, the debts of that department were growing at an alarming rate, reaching a figure in the region of £200,000 by the end of the reign.[36] The sale of some of the royal jewels would certainly have helped the officials of the wardrobe to balance their books, but the king evidently did not think it his duty to dispose permanently of a substantial part of his jewels, whatever their provenance, to this end. The only concession he made to ease in a very small way the financial burden imposed on his government by the military ventures of the last decade of his reign was to pledge some of his jewels in Brabant in 1297 as a security for the repayment of a loan of 4,000 *livres de petits tournois noirs* (£1,000 at the contemporary rate of exchange). The pledged jewels, which consisted of 186 gems, mostly sapphires and rubies, contained in thirty staffs (*baculi*), and of several objects adorned with precious stones, namely one gold comb, one gold brooch, one gold crown, one gold cross, and one large chaplet, were valued by the money-lenders at 7,015 *livres de petits tournois noirs* (approximately £1,754). They were returned from Brabant at Edward II's coronation except for the gold cross, which the friar-preacher Nicholas de Wisbech was sent to Brabant to retrieve from Duke John III in January 1318.[37]

[35] *Liber Quot.*, p. 349.

[36] Michael Prestwich, *War, Politics, and Finance under Edward I* (London, 1972), p. 221. Compare Tout, *Chapters*, ii. 125.

[37] PRO E 159/71, m. 36 (*Documents Illustrating the Crisis of 1297–1298 in England*, ed. Michael Prestwich (Royal Historical Society, Camden 4th Series, xxiv, 1980), no. 206); see Hamilton in *Albion*, 23 (1991), 202 n. 5. For the letters of credence of Nicholas de Wisbech, see PRO C 70/4, m. 13d (8 Jan. 1318): 'Rex nobili viro domino Johanni duci Brabanc', Lottric' et Lymburg' comiti, nepoti suo karissimo, salutem et sincere dileccionis affectum. De fidelitate et circumspeccione provida religiosi viri et nobis in Cristo dilecti fratris Nicholai de Wysebeche, de ordine predicatorum, latoris presencium, plenam fiduciam optinentes, ipsum ad vos duximus destinandum, vos attencius deprecantes quatinus illam crucem auream, que una cum aliis jocalibus celebris memorie domini E. genitoris nostri ad manus domini J. patris vestri ex certis causis devenit et que, restitutis nobis nuper in coronacione nostra dictis jocalibus, penes eundem

There were numerous occasions on which medieval rulers gave jewels as presents and were expected to do so. Edward I was no exception. A royal visit to a holy shrine, for example that of Our Lady at Walsingham, of St Etheldreda at Ely, of St Hugh at Lincoln, of St John at Beverley, or of St Thomas at Canterbury, called for an offering, which in Edward's case often consisted of a gold brooch.[38] According to an old-established tradition, especially rich jewels were sent to a new pope on the occasion of his coronation, a practice which Edward I never failed to observe.[39] Foreign envoys on a diplomatic mission to England were also often presented with jewels before returning home,[40] as were sometimes lesser persons such as couriers who had brought pleasing news from a foreign ruler.[41] Had these numerous gifts been taken out of the 'old store' of wardrobe jewels, they would soon have exhausted the royal treasure. For that reason, the wardrobe purchased from time to time a large number of jewels, thus forming a new stock from which royal gifts were almost invariably drawn.[42] A few exceptions have been noted, but they are as rare as they are remarkable. Out of several precious objects presented by Philip IV to Edward I in France in 1286, only one gold cup was deposited in the wardrobe. None of the others ever reached the royal treasure; they were distributed forthwith ('incontinenti'): a gold crown was sent to the king's daughter Eleanor in England; two cloths of gold were given to the king's consort, Eleanor of Castile, and a gold

patrem vestrum remansit et ad vos postmodum devenit, ut intelleximus, dicto fratri Nicholao liberetis ad nos deferendam, prout sibi injunximus oretenus, sibi in hiis que de cruce predicta et que nos et vos contingunt ex parte nostra exposuerit viva voce fidem credulam adhibentes, ea sicut negocia vos contingencia per nos prosperari desideratis opere compleatis, dicto fratri Nicholao pro se et ejus familia litteras vestras de salvo et securo conductu in competenti et speciali forma, prout vos requisierit, concedendo ac quid super premissis feceritis nobis per eundem, si placet, rescribendo. Dat' ut supra [sc. apud Westm' viij die januarii]'. Wisbech also had letters of credence of the same date addressed to the pope (PRO C 70/4, m. 13d).

[38] *Liber Quot.*, p. 334.

[39] In a letter of 2 Mar. 1304 to Walter Langton, Edward I explained that he did not intend to make any request to the pope 'tant qil nous eit signefie son noun et la novele de sa creacion et qe nous li eons fait puis present de beaux joeaux, ne il ne afferreit mie . . . ne nentendons mie qe autrement eit este usez cea en arieres en temps de nous ne de nos ancestres, ne nous ne bions cel usage changer' (Chaplais, *EMDP* I. ii, no. 319). For presents sent to the pope by Edward I and Edward II, see ibid., no. 409 and p. 818 nn. 7–8.

[40] Chaplais, *EMDP* I. ii, nos. 406, 407, 411.

[41] Ibid., no. 406; *Liber Quot.*, p. 339. For messengers bringing letters, however, gifts of money were more usual; see Chaplais, *EMDP* I. ii, notes to pp. 821, 823.

[42] *Liber Quot.*, pp. 335–42.

brooch to the knight John de Vile.[43] On 11 September 1299 in Canterbury, on the occasion of his marriage to his second wife Margaret, Edward gave his new bride several jewels which had belonged to Blanche of France (or 'of Spain'), namely a gold crown, a gold coronet, and a gold belt, all adorned with precious stones.[44] In 1304 a gold ring with a balas ruby, which had belonged to Godfrey Giffard, late bishop of Worcester, and had been delivered into the wardrobe by his executors on 21 April 1302 at Devizes, was presented by Edward to Walter de Winterbourne, his confessor, when the latter was created cardinal priest of S. Sabina.[45] Although it could be said that Blanche's jewels and Bishop Giffard's ring already belonged to the royal treasure when they were given respectively to Queen Margaret and to Winterbourne, they were recent acquisitions. The 'old store' of the wardrobe had not been affected.

Gaveston, the chamberlainship, and the custody of the king's jewels

Having survived nearly unscathed the costly wars of Edward I and the Westminster burglary of 1303, the royal treasure had totally disappeared at the beginning of the next reign, or so the Ordinances of 1311 claimed. The culprit was Gaveston, who had appropriated the whole treasure and sent it out of the kingdom ('en acoillaunt a lui tout le tresor le roi et lad esloigne hors du roiaume').[46] True or false, the story was too good not to be exploited by chroniclers biased against Gaveston; Trokelowe, for example, who was quite sure that the jewels and other goods seized in Newcastle in 1312 had been left there by Gaveston ('que dictus Petrus . . . dimiserat') and had been taken from him by Lancaster and his adherents ('que a dicto Petro . . . capiebant'),[47] could be expected to improve on the story he found in the Ordinances. According to him, Gaveston had started appropriating 'the treasure and jewels of the realm' in Edward I's lifetime, taking whatever part of it the prince of Wales had and giving it to foreign merchants to keep for him. After his return from Ireland in 1309, his

---

[43] *Records of the Wardrobe and Household, 1285–1286*, ed. B. F. Byerly and C. R. Byerly (HMSO, 1977), no. 2004.　　　　　　　　　　　　　　　　[44] PRO E 101/355/26.
[45] BL MS Add. 8835, fo. 123ʳ.
[46] *Rot. Parl.* i. 283; *Statutes*, i. 162; *BIHR* 57 (1984), 201.
[47] Trokelowe, pp. 75, 78.

appropriation of the royal treasure increased and once again the loot was entrusted to foreign merchants.[48] The author of the 'Chronicle of the Civil Wars of Edward II' does not involve foreign merchants in Gaveston's pillage of the royal treasury. He emphasizes instead the king's ultimate responsibility for it and the disastrous effects it had not only for the king himself, but also for the English people:

He granted and gave away to the same Piers the old treasures and precious jewels which his ancestors had from time immemorial placed for safety in the king's treasury at Westminster; he did so to his own shame and to the greatest prejudice of himself and of the whole English people, because, as soon as he had exhausted his own treasure, he needed the help of the people and he imposed taxes upon them. Thus he extorted and levied large sums of money to the impoverishment of his people.[49]

Walter of Guisborough, too, had no doubt about Edward II's connivance in Gaveston's depredations, which started when Edward was prince of Wales. From what the chronicler says we gather that the two adoptive brothers had made excessive demands on Edward I's treasure and that Walter Langton, at the time royal treasurer, had refused to comply. When the old king died, his successor and Gaveston took their revenge on Langton, who was arrested and his own treasure seized to the value of £50,000, not to mention much gold, jewels, and precious stones, which the new king gave Gaveston. (Ironically, a privy seal writ of 27 November 1307, unknown to Guisborough, accused Langton of having appropriated a large amount ('grant foison') of the late king's treasure.)[50] Both Edward and Gaveston were present when Langton's chests, which were found in the New Temple in London, where they were hidden, were broken into. This had been done even before Edward I had been laid to rest. The new king also gave the whole treasure of his father to Gaveston, that is to say £100,000 as well as gold, precious stones, and many

[48] Trokelowe, pp. 64–5, 68.

[49] BL MS Cotton Cleopatra D ix, fo. 86ʳ (*Speculum*, 14 (1939), 75–6): 'Antiquos thesauros et preciosa jocalia in gazophilacio regis apud Westm' per suos antecessores a tempore a quo non extitit memoria salvo depositos eidem Petro contulit et distribuit in proprium dedecus et dampnum gravissimum sui ipsius et tocius populi Anglicani, quia, exhausto thesauro suo proprio, statim indigebat auxilio populari talliagiaque eis imposuit. Sic pecuniam extorsit et levare fecit non modicam ad depaupcracionem gentis sue.'

[50] Conway Davies, *Baron. Opp.*, p. 547.

jewels, nearly all of which Piers sent to his native Gascony ('transmisit in patriam suam') through the intermediary of merchants.[51]

Whether in their succinct form as in the Ordinances or in their more elaborate version as in the chronicles, the charges against Gaveston that he had appropriated all the royal treasure and sent it abroad, unsupported as they are by any record evidence, cannot be taken seriously. How could the earl of Lancaster claim in 1311, as one of the Ordainers, that Gaveston had taken all the royal treasure out of the country, and argue in 1312–13 that the impressive collection of valuable royal jewels which he had found in Newcastle was a Gaveston hoard? Nor can the charges against Gaveston be reconciled with the indubitable fact that c.2 October 1311, at about the time of publication of the Ordinances, the king still had enough jewels stored in Westminster to need a boat for their transport to the Tower of London.[52] This does not necessarily mean that the Ordainers as well as Trokelowe, Guisborough, and the anonymous author of the 'Chronicle of the Civil Wars of Edward II' all lied deliberately. More probably, they misinterpreted some piece of evidence which established a link of some kind between Gaveston and the royal treasure. Here again, as in the matter of the Westminster gifts,[53] Gaveston's possible holding of the office of chief chamberlain may be the connection.

Let us turn once more to the *Vita*, which states in its fourth sentence that Gaveston had been the 'camerarius familiarissimus et ualde dilectus' of Edward of Carnarvon as prince of Wales.[54] Because of the use of the superlative 'familiarissimus', one has to concede to T. F. Tout and other modern writers that here the word 'camerarius' cannot refer to the holder of an office which was unique.[55] Of all the officers of Edward's chamber Gaveston was closest to the prince and well loved by him, but he was not necessarily the head of his chamber or 'camerarius' in the restricted sense of the word. In the end, however, the distinction may amount to little more than hair-splitting, since it is unlikely that the prince would have allowed his favourite cameral officer to remain in a subordinate position for long,

[51] Guisborough, p. 383.
[52] BL MS Cotton Nero C viii, fo. 82ᵛ, printed above, n. 27.
[53] See above, ch. 3.   [54] *Vita*, p. 1.
[55] Conway Davies, *Baron. Opp.*, p. 99 n. 4; Tout, *Place of Edw. II*, p. 11 n. 3; *Vita*, p. 1 n. 2.

particularly if we take into account the further remark in the *Vita* that Gaveston's services in the household of the prince were so much appreciated that in a short time he reached 'the peak of his lord's highest favour' ('summi fauoris apicem optinuit in breui').[56] These comments in the *Vita*, combined with the documentary evidence of gifts from the abbot of Westminster to both Gaveston and Charlton in November 1306,[57] give us at least a legitimate excuse for suggesting that by that time Gaveston, once merely one of a group of chamberlains in the sense of officers of the prince's chamber, had through merit risen to the enviable post of chamberlain-in-chief.

What the *Vita* says about Gaveston's status in the chamber of Edward of Carnarvon as king still falls short of the conclusive proof which we should like to have, but only by a small margin: 'If an earl or baron who wished to speak with the king entered the royal chamber, in the presence of Piers the king would neither speak to nor smile at anybody except Piers.'[58] This may be a distorted version of what really happened: perhaps the king would not answer the earls or barons except in Gaveston's presence and then only through the latter's mouth, following the practice of many medieval rulers, who did not reply to formal messages in person, but did so through an intermediary speaking in their presence.[59] It was also one of the complaints made in 1312 against Hugh le Despenser the younger, royal chamberlain, and his father that they would neither allow magnates or good councillors to speak to the king or approach him to give him good counsel, nor let the king speak to them, save in their presence.[60] In the late-fourteenth and early-fifteenth centuries, it was not unusual for the intermediary between the king and petitioners to be the royal chamberlain, who either signed or endorsed the petitions which had been granted.[61] If we trust the annalist of St Paul's, Gaveston would have exercised similar functions between 1307 and 1312:

There are various kinds of favours which, by virtue of the royal prerogative, it properly belongs to the king and to no one else to bestow on his subjects.

---

[56] *Vita*, p. 14.
[57] Harvey, *Wenlok*, I, no. 227, and p. 201; above, ch. 3.   [58] *Vita*, p. 15.
[59] Chaplais, *EMDP* I. i. 110–11 n. 205.
[60] Michael Prestwich, 'The Charges against the Despensers, 1321', *BIHR* 58 (1985), 98.
[61] Maxwell-Lyte, *Great Seal*, pp. 145, 152; A. L. Brown, 'The Authorization of Letters under the Great Seal', *BIHR* 37 (1964), 134–5, 148–9; Conway Davies, *Baron. Opp.*, p. 215.

Those were in practice granted by the king to Piers, since, whenever an earl or magnate had a special royal favour to request on some business, the king sent him on to Piers, whose word and decision would soon be put into effect and agreed by the king. Everybody was indignant that there should thus be two kings reigning together in one kingdom, one in name and the other in deed.[62]

The annalist goes further still, stating positively that Gaveston was royal chamberlain: Edward II would have made him 'secretary' and high chamberlain of the realm ('secretarium et camerarium regni summum') before granting him the earldom of Cornwall.[63]

If the appointment to the chamberlainship was the king's personal decision, as it must have been, it was probably made when the two adoptive brothers met again after Gaveston's return from his exile in Ponthieu; if so, it cannot have preceded the issue of the charter of 6 August 1307, which had granted him the earldom of Cornwall in his absence; a date between Gaveston's return and the Northampton parliament of Michaelmas 1307 in which the charter was confirmed seems more plausible.[64] The *camerarius familiarissimus* of the former prince of Wales[65] had now been promoted to the rank of high chamberlain of the realm.[66]

If Gaveston really was the king's chamberlain, as the younger Despenser was to be in the second half of the reign, this would have given him the opportunity of promoting members of his own household from the stable to the king's chamber, as the *Vita* claims that he did.[67] He did not usurp his control of royal patronage;[68] he exercised it with the king's assent in his capacity as royal chamberlain.

---

[62] *Ann. Paul.*, p. 259: 'Rex diversa genera gratiarum erga subditos, que ex prerogativa regia proprie sibi soli et non alii incumbebant, in opere contulit illi Petro. Nam si quis ex comitibus aut ex magnatibus haberet requirere specialem gratiam regis super aliquo negotio expediendo, rex cum mitteret ad Petrum; et quod ille diceret aut preciperet, mox fieret; et rex etiam acceptaret. Unde indignatus est populus universus duos reges in uno regno, istum verbaliter, istum realiter conregnare.' For the remark made by Robert of Avesbury that the younger Despenser, later on in the reign, behaved like a second king ('ut alter rex'), see Conway Davies, *Baron. Opp.*, p. 104 n. 6.   [63] *Ann. Paul.*, p. 258.   [64] *Lanercost*, p. 210.

[65] *Vita*, p. 1.

[66] By 'high chamberlain of the realm', the expression used by the *Annales Paulini*, we should understand, of course, 'royal chamberlain', not 'chamberlain of England'. For Geoffrey le Baker's statement that Hugh le Despenser the younger was made 'camerarius regis loco Petri', see Tout, *Place of Edw. II*, p. 11 n. 3. If Baker is right, it follows not only that the appointment of Despenser would have taken place as early as 1312, but also that Gaveston had been his predecessor in the office.   [67] *Vita*, p. 29.

[68] See Maddicott, *Lancaster*, pp. 78–9, 89; Hamilton, *Gaveston*, pp. 44–5.

As the titular head of the king's chamber, Gaveston was nominally responsible for all the transactions of the department, including those connected with the custody of forfeited lands and the disposal of forfeited chattels, matters which in the previous reign had apparently been handled by the wardrobe, but were some time after 1307 transferred to the chamber.[69] We can now begin to make sense of the claim advanced by the *Annales Paulini* that Walter Langton's treasure, horses, and cattle were 'given' to Gaveston;[70] the truth probably was that they had been handed over to him not as a private person for his own benefit, but in his official capacity as chamberlain, so that they would be kept safe for the king's use. We may even accept as not implausible the assertion in the same Annals that in late January or early February 1308 Philip IV's wedding presents were sent forthwith (from France) by Edward to Gaveston.[71] Instead of being another illustration of Edward's alleged habit of lavishing valuable presents on Gaveston, it was simply designed to ensure the safe keeping of the gifts by sending them without delay to the royal chamberlain, who also happened to be at the time keeper of the realm. It was not meant as an insult to Philip IV,[72] nor could it be construed as such except perhaps by the English barons; on the contrary, it was a mark of appreciation. Whether it was in his capacity as royal chamberlain that Gaveston redeemed the Curtana sword at the coronation[73] is a matter for speculation; perhaps it was at any rate one of his duties to return the sword to a safe place after it had served its purpose at the ceremony.

There is no doubt that, by the second half of Edward II's reign, the chamber had become an important repository for the king's jewels, another encroachment on the functions of the wardrobe.[74] For the

[69] Tout, *Chapters*, ii. 316–17. For forfeited jewels in the wardrobe in 1299–1300, see *Liber Quot.*, p. 343.   [70] *Ann. Paul.*, p. 257.   [71] Ibid., p. 258.

[72] Conway Davies, *Baron. Opp.*, p. 84; Maddicott, *Lancaster*, p. 83; Elizabeth A. R. Brown in *Speculum*, 63 (1988), 582 n. 19; Hamilton in *Albion*, 23 (1991), 202, 205 n. 22. Sending Philip's gifts to the chamberlain for safe keeping could hardly be compared to Edward I's immediate disposal of some of Philip's presents in 1286; see above, n. 43.

[73] *Foedera*: R. II. i. 36.

[74] J. Conway Davies, 'The First Journal of Edward II's Chamber', *EHR* 30 (1915), 668; Tout, *Chapters*, ii. 328, 338 n. 4, 339, 344 n. 4, 353, 357. For the position in Edward I's reign, see *Fleta*, ed. H. G. Richardson and G. O. Sayles, ii (Selden Society, lxxii, 1955), 126 (bk. 2, ch. 14): 'Officium autem thesaurarii garderobe est: pecuniam, iocalia et exennia regi facta recipere, recepta regisque secreta custodire'.

period preceding Gaveston's death, the record evidence, although slim, is adequate enough to show that already jewels were from time to time transferred from the wardrobe to the chamber. On 3 April 1311 from Berwick-upon-Tweed, for example, the king ordered some brooches, rings, and other jewels to be delivered out of the wardrobe to James of Audley (yeoman of the king's chamber), to be kept by him in the king's presence ('ad custodiendum in presencia ipsius regis').[75]

Whereas the Ordinances of 1311 accuse Gaveston unequivocally of having appropriated all the royal treasure, the author of the Annals of London and even Robert of Reading are far less emphatic. In so far as both of them are concerned, it was not of appropriating the treasure that Gaveston was guilty, but of squandering it after it had been entrusted to his care by the king. According to the Annals, Edward had left all the royal treasure, jewels, and precious stones to the disposal and will of Piers, who as head of the royal house ('regiam domum tenens') spared no expense,[76] while Robert of Reading accuses Gaveston of having impoverished the king by squandering the royal treasures committed to his charge.[77] Neither the London annalist nor Robert of Reading specifies in what capacity Gaveston was placed in charge of the royal treasure, but the annalist comes close to it when he refers to the Gascon as 'regiam domum tenens', an expression practically synonymous with the title of 'secretarius et camerarius regni summus' given to him by the Annales Paulini.[78]

Whether under Gaveston's nominal chamberlainship and John Charlton's effective subchamberlainship the expenditure of the chamber was extravagant or not, it is impossible to say, because there are no chamber accounts for the period preceding the 1320s.[79] To help with its finances, the chamber may well have disposed of royal jewels, in the same way as, in the first year of the reign, gold cloths,

[75] Bodl. Lib. MS Tanner 197, fos. 62ᵛ, 63ʳ. For Audley, see Conway Davies, Baron. Opp., p. 197; Tout, Chapters, ii. 320.
[76] Ann. Lond., p. 151. The annalist refers to the treasure captured by the earl of Lancaster in Newcastle on 4 May 1312 as the king's treasure ('cepit thesaurum regis'; ibid., p. 204).
[77] Flores, iii. 142.   [78] Ann. Paul., p. 258.
[79] It is difficult to know how far there were separate accounts of the chamber between 1307 and 1312. At that time, some of the finances of the chamber may have been handled by the wardrobe, whose keeper and treasurer was Ingelard de Warle, one of the king's creatures and one of the barons' bêtes noires. For Warle, see Ann. Lond., p. 200; Conway Davies, Baron. Opp., p. 384; Tout, Place of Edw. II, pp. 73, 92; Tout, Chapters, ii. 317–19.

plate, and jewels were sold for £1,250 12s. 11d. to supplement the receipts of the wardrobe under John de Benstede as keeper.[80]

What happened to the chamberlainship when Gaveston was away from England during his second and third exiles is unknown; while he was in Ireland, John Charlton, his deputy, was also away, having gone into exile with him.[81] We can only assume that, in Edward's eyes, the post of chamberlain, like the earldom of Cornwall, never ceased to be Gaveston's and that he resumed whatever official duties were involved as soon as he came back. This is perhaps what the canon of Bridlington tried to convey to his readers when he wrote that, when Gaveston returned to England in January 1312, 'he attached himself to the king as before, and he was made royal secretary' (*domino regi sicut prius adhesit, ipsiusque secretarius est effectus*);[82] it is unfortunate that the meaning of *secretarius* in this context should be far from clear.[83]

If Gaveston was still in charge of the royal jewels when, early in May 1312, he fled from Newcastle, leaving everything behind, his flight was little short of a desertion of duty in the face of the enemy, but he was in the company of Edward, who must have insisted on this indecorous retreat.

We have already given our reasons for believing that the royal jewels seized by the earl of Lancaster in Newcastle were still truly the king's rather than a Gaveston hoard of stolen property. That they were stored together with the goods of Gaveston himself needs no further explanation, if he really held the post of head of the king's chamber and as such was responsible for the custody of the royal jewels in his department. But how did it happen that so many valuable items were allowed to travel with the king around the country instead of being stored in a safe place such as the Tower of London or even in the now discredited treasury at Westminster? The clue to this puzzle should perhaps be sought in the considerable restrictions which the Ordinances of 1311 imposed on the king's

---

[80] Tout, *Chapters*, ii. 361: 'De pannis aureis, vessellamentis, petrariis, coclearis, ciphis, florenis et aliis jocalibus venditis, £1,250. 12. 11.'

[81] *CPR 1307–1313*, p. 80.   [82] *Bridlington*, p. 42.

[83] Hugh le Despenser the younger, royal chamberlain, was described in a great seal writ of 22 Nov. 1323 as the king's 'secretary', but so were others at the same time. See L. B. Dibben, 'Secretaries in the Thirteenth and Fourteenth Centuries', *EHR* 25 (1910), 431; Chaplais, *EMDP* I. i. 337; see also Conway Davies, *Baron. Opp.*, p. 104 n. 2.

financial resources. Edward may have thought that the time would soon come when he would need to find easy access to ready cash and bypass the baronial control over the exchequer. It cannot have escaped him that one way of achieving this objective would be to dispose of some of his valuable jewels or at least pawn them, however regrettable either solution might be. When the king had a boat-load of jewels taken from Westminster to the Tower of London by the master of the royal barge *la Swallow c.*2 October 1311,[84] was it really because he was concerned about their safety? The timing of the transfer, very close to the date of publication of the Ordinances, cannot fail to arouse suspicion, and one cannot help wondering whether the jewels in question were not precisely those which Thomas of Lancaster found in Newcastle.

Concrete evidence has been produced above that some of the Newcastle jewels had almost certainly belonged to the store of the wardrobe as it was in Edward I's reign.[85] From the description of the majority of the other royal items in Lancaster's inventory it may be inferred that they had also belonged there. Only a few jewels in the list had been given to Edward II himself either before or after his accession, for example the gold cup bequeathed to him by Eleanor of Castile, his mother,[86] one brooch given to him by his sister Elizabeth (*Isabelle*),[87] one gold brooch presented by John de Leek, his former chaplain and almoner when he was prince of Wales,[88] and two other gold brooches, which Queen Isabella had given him.[89] The rest had belonged to the royal wardrobe in Edward I's time, two late items being one sapphire and one silver cup which had belonged to Bishop Gilbert of St Leofard of Chichester[90] and had presumably been delivered into the wardrobe shortly after his death on 12 February 1305.[91] Since, on the one hand, none of the jewels in Lancaster's list can be identified with any of those remaining in the wardrobe on 31 January 1311,[92] and, on the other, Lancaster's list does not include

---

[84] See above, n. 27.

[86] Below, App. II, item 87.

[88] Ibid., item 18; see Tout, *Chapters*, ii. 171.

[90] Ibid., items 65, 109.

[85] See above, nn. 9–19.

[87] Ibid., item 19.

[89] Below, App. II, items 22, 23.

[91] John Le Neve, *Fasti Ecclesiae Anglicanae, 1300–1541*, vii (Chichester Diocese), comp. Joyce M. Horn (Athlone Press, London, 1964), p. 1.

[92] Bodl. Lib. MS Tanner 197, fos. 61ᵛ–63ᵛ.

three gold rings which the executors of dead prelates brought into the wardrobe on 3 December 1307, 12 January 1308, and 25 December 1308 respectively, and which were still there on 31 January 1311,[93] it follows that the Newcastle jewels cannot have been those of the itinerant store of the wardrobe. The conclusion that they were kept in the chamber and that they had been originally the wardrobe jewels transported from Westminster to the Tower of London *c*.2 October 1311 can hardly be avoided. Edward may have removed them from the Tower some time between 2 October and his departure for the north after Christmas. They would then have come under Gaveston's care after his return from Flanders in January 1312.

[93] The rings were those of Thomas Bitton, bishop of Exeter, Walter de Wenlok, abbot of Westminster, and Walter Haselshaw, bishop of Bath (ibid., fo. 62^r).

CONCLUSION

ADOPTIVE BROTHERS
OR LOVERS?

No record evidence has been found which can be said to prove conclusively that, in the early days of his relationship with Gaveston, Edward of Carnarvon contracted with him a compact of adoptive brotherhood, be it brotherhood-in-arms or some other kind of fraternity. To be conclusive, the evidence would have to consist of a text of the compact, but written agreements of adoptive brotherhood have seldom survived. The existence of such a bond, however, is supported by a great deal of circumstantial evidence, besides being a more plausible explanation for the preferential treatment which, on one occasion after another, Gaveston received from Edward as king, than the gratuitous assumption that they were lovers. The grant to Gaveston of the earldom of Cornwall, his appointment as keeper of the realm, as royal lieutenant in Ireland, and as royal chamberlain, as well as the special part he played in the coronation ceremony, all these favours were consistent with adoptive brotherhood. Edward went as far as a king could go to share his worldly advantages with his brother, and indeed he went too far in that direction in the opinion of those contemporaries who thought that Gaveston was treated by him and behaved as a second king or nearly so ('quasi secundus rex').[1]

Perhaps Edward did not make as much effort as he ought to have done to secure his adoptive brother's release when he was captured in May 1312, but if Robert of Reading is right in claiming that the king gave £1,000 to the earl of Pembroke to induce him to take charge of Gaveston, was this just a bribe or was it meant to be an advance

[1] *Vita*, p. 1.

payment on the ransom which brothers-in-arms were supposed to raise for one another in the event of capture by an enemy?[2] At least, after Gaveston's death, his widow Margaret de Clare and his daughter Joan were well looked after by the king, who acted as generously towards them as was expected of the surviving brother-in-arms, providing a comfortable life for both as well as a suitable education and marriage for Joan.[3]

The relationship between Edward and Gaveston was unusual enough to make a man like the author of the *Vita*, well read in the classics and in the Bible, search for precedents and analogies in his past readings. There was, of course, the partnership between Jonathan and David. The author of the *Vita* does not go beyond saying that Edward's love for Gaveston resembled that of Jonathan for David.[4] But there may have been others who pursued the parallel further and saw something politically sinister in Edward's association with Gaveston: Jonathan had proposed that David should be king and that he, Jonathan, would be 'second' to him.[5] Had Edward come to a similar arrangement with Gaveston? According to the annalist of St Paul's, it was the general view that he had: 'Everyone was indignant', he wrote, 'that there should be two kings reigning jointly in one kingdom, one in name and the other in deed.'[6]

There was also the partnership of Achilles and Patroclus. Again, the author of the *Vita* refers to it casually.[7] But there was a strange similarity between the funeral arrangements made by Achilles for Patroclus and those made by Edward for Gaveston. Achilles had waited to perform the funeral rites for his friend until he had avenged his death; Gaveston was murdered on 19 June 1312, but Edward waited for two and a half years before he had Gaveston buried; the ceremony took place in King's Langley on 2 January 1315.[8] At the time of his death, of course, Gaveston was still an excommunicate; as such he could not be buried in consecrated ground unless there was proof that he had repented before death for whatever sins he was supposed to have committed. The postponement of the burial may be

---

[2] *Flores*, iii. 150–1; Maddicott, *Lancaster*, p. 126.
[3] Conway Davies, *Baron. Opp.*, pp. 85–6; Hamilton, *Gaveston*, pp. 101–2.
[4] *Vita*, pp. 15, 30.   [5] 1 Sam. 23: 17.
[6] *Annal. Paul.*, p. 259. See above, ch. 5 n. 62.   [7] *Vita*, p. 15.
[8] For the date, see Phillips, *Pembroke*, p. 83; Hallam, *Itinerary*, p. 122.

explained in this way, but why was the burial with all religious rites finally allowed in January 1315, although there is no evidence that the sentence of excommunication was ever lifted? Perhaps Edward was waiting for Archbishop Winchelsey's death, which eventually occurred on 11 May 1313.[9] But the body of Gaveston still remained unburied for another nineteen months, one year after the enthronement of Winchelsey's successor, Walter Reynolds, who had been Gaveston's friend and ally.[10] The author of the *Vita* explains that there was a rumour that Edward had wished to take revenge on Gaveston's murderers before committing his body to the ground, but he had changed his mind because those from whom he sought vengeance had been 'readmitted to friendship'.[11] It certainly is true that those guilty of murdering Gaveston were pardoned, but the pardons were issued in October 1313,[12] long before Gaveston's burial. Apparently not everyone was satisfied that the king had given up revenge, and when the earl of Warwick died in August 1315, there were many, we are told, who suspected foul play and thought that he had been poisoned.[13] Even if this is true, however, and if the king had anything to do with Warwick's death, it happened too late to explain the timing of Gaveston's burial. What may be significant is that 2 January, the date chosen for the funeral, fell within the octaves of the Innocents, a point which would have appealed to Edward: what had Piers done which merited death?

In the meantime a curious incident had occurred in 1313 as recorded in the following payment made by the wardrobe in the sixth year of the king's reign:

To Richard de Neueby, a yeoman from Gascony, who says that he is the king's brother, of the king's gift, by the hands of the said Roger who delivered the money to him at Eltham on 22 May, £13.[14]

Thus, it seems, a certain yeoman from Gascony, who called himself Richard de Neueby (a curious name for a Gascon), appeared in the royal court at Eltham in Kent on 22 May 1313, saying that he was

---

[9] *Brit. Chron.*, p. 233. [10] Ibid. [11] *Vita*, pp. 58–9.
[12] Maddicott, *Lancaster*, p. 150. [13] *Speculum*, 14 (1939), 77.
[14] PRO E 101/375/8, fo. 29d: 'Ricardo de Neueby, valletto de Vasconia, dicenti se esse fratrem regis, de dono ipsius regis per manus dicti domini Rogeri liberantis ei denarios apud Eltham xxij die maii, xiij li.' The *Rogerus* who delivered the money has not been identified.

the king's brother. Did he claim to be a blood-brother, in other words an illegitimate son of Edward I, or an adoptive brother as Gaveston had been? Was he a madman like those who from time to time went around the country pretending to be the true king?[15] If he too was an impostor, his crime was not as great as theirs, but it seems incredible that, instead of being thrown into prison, tried, and punished, he received from the king a gift of £13, which for a man of his station, a yeoman (*vallettus*), represented the wages of 260 days.[16] This does not necessarily mean, however, that his claim was believed to be true. Richard had called at the royal court, either by accident or by design, at a most inconvenient time, when the king and his wife Isabella were getting ready to go to France; they sailed on the next day, 23 May.[17] A scandal at that juncture would have been disastrous.

Our discussion of the institution of adoptive brotherhood in England began with the treaty of Alney concluded in 1016 between Edmund Ironside and Cnut, a treaty which, according to some chronicles, led to the murder of Edmund. In the twelfth century, there were rumours, known to William of Malmesbury and Henry of Huntingdon as well as to the compiler of the *Liber Eliensis*, that the murder had been perpetrated in a particularly vile fashion.[18] If we trust Geoffrey le Baker, who wrote his chronicle a generation or so after Edward II's death, and the still later Meaux chronicler, Edward would also have suffered a horrible death, strangely similar to that of

---

[15] See *Vita*, pp. 86–7; *Ann. Paul.*, pp. 282–3; *Bridlington*, p. 55; Johnstone, *Edw. of Carnarvon*, pp. 130–1.   [16] Ibid., p. 74 n. 4.

[17] *Gascon Rolls*, iv, ed. Y. Renouard, p. xiv.

[18] Henry of Huntingdon, p. 186: 'Cum rex hostibus suis terribilis et timendissimus in regno floreret, ivit nocte quadam in domum evacuationis ad requisita nature, ubi filius Edrici ducis in fovea secretaria delitescens consilio patris, regem inter celanda cultello bis acuto percussit; et inter viscera ferrum figens, fugiens reliquit'; William of Malmesbury, *Gesta Regum*, i. 217: 'Fama Edricum infamat, quod favore alterius mortem ei per ministros porrexerit; cubicularios regis fuisse duos, quibus omnem vitam suam commiserat: quos pollicitationibus illectos, et primo immanitatem flagitii exhorrentes, brevi complices suos effecisse; ejus consilio ferreum uncum, ad nature requisita sedenti, in locis posterioribus adegisse'; see also *Liber Eliensis*, ed. E. O. Blake (Royal Historical Society, Camden 3rd Series, xcii, 1962), p. 148: 'rex Ædmundus rediens Lundoniam, perimitur dolo predicti Ædrici veru ferreo in secreta nature transfixus, dum in secessu sederet'. Godfrey II, duke of Lower Lorraine, is said to have been murdered in the same way in 1076; see G. H. Pertz, *Scriptores Rerum Germanicarum*, xvi (Hanover, 1859), 603: 'Ducem Godefridum gibbosum sicarius interimit, cultello feriens per secreta nature, dum ad purgandum alvum in secessum sederet'; *Two of the Saxon Chronicles Parallel*, ed. Plummer, ii. 199–200. For other examples of similar murders, see E. A. Freeman, *The History of the Norman Conquest of England*, i (3rd edn. Oxford, 1877), 716.

Edmund.[19] Perhaps neither of these stories is true, but those who might be tempted to connect the manner of Edward's death, as described by Baker and the Meaux chronicler, with his alleged practice of sodomy would find it difficult to extend the same interpretation to the case of Edmund Ironside. The only possible connection between Edmund and Edward II is that both appear to have been involved in a compact of adoptive brotherhood and that, in both cases, the compact was widely resented as believed to be contrary to the country's general interest. It was obviously the sort of agreement into which it was unwise for a king or the heir to the throne to enter, but in Edward's case we may wonder whether it was the principle of the agreement which aroused objections or rather the personality of the king's partner. If he had chosen to adopt as his brother a 'more suitable' companion of his youth such as Gilbert, heir to the earldom of Gloucester and connected with the royal line, instead of a foreigner who, although no commoner, was neither of royal descent nor even of a high-baronial line, the relationship might have caused less resentment and jealousy. It was not in any case the relationship in itself which was resented as much as its repercussions in the political and constitutional fields, and the favours which it brought Gaveston, notably the grant of the chamberlainship, which enabled him to control royal patronage and all matters connected with the king's prerogative.

It may be argued that Edward and Gaveston could have been lovers as well as adoptive brothers, but there is no specific reference in any contemporary chronicle to such a relationship. Even if there was, we should treat it with caution, remembering that this was an age in which false charges of sodomy had been fabricated against Boniface VIII and the grand master of the Templars, Philip the Fair's enemies. The claim of the Meaux chronicler that Edward indulged in the vice

[19] *Chronicon Galfridi le Baker de Swynebroke*, ed. E. M. Thompson (Oxford, 1889), p. 33: 'in lecto cubantem subito preocupatum, cum pulvinaribus magnis atque gravi mole amplius quam quindecim robustorum ipsum oppressum et subfocatum, cum ferro plumbarii incense ignito trans tubam ductilem ad egestionis partes secretas applicatam membra spiritalia post intestinas combusserunt'. See also Higden, *Polychronicon*, viii. 324: 'cum veru ignito inter celanda confossus ignominiose peremptus est'; *Melsa*, ii. 355: 'dum a prandio surgere deberet, mensa in qua edebat depressus fuit, et cum veru ferreo candente inter celanda confossus nefarie peremptus est'; G. P. Cuttino and Thomas W. Lyman, 'Where is Edward II?', *Speculum*, 53 (1978), 524. Only for Edward II's murder was a red-hot weapon used.

of sodomy excessively[20] is likely to have been based solely on the remark commonly found in chronicles of the reign that he loved Gaveston 'beyond measure' (*ultra modum*).[21] Had the same Meaux chronicler read Roger de Aldenham's letter of 25 May 1309 in which Gaveston is said to have loved the earl of Richmond also beyond measure, he would no doubt have accused Richmond (who happened to be unmarried) of the same sin.[22] If we in our turn wish to interpret as an accusation of sodomy the statement in the *Annales Paulini* that there was a rumour going around the country that the king loved an evil male sorcerer more than he did his wife, we might equally aim the same charge at David, who valued Jonathan's love more than he did the love of women.[23]

---

[20] *Melsa*, ii. 355.   [21] *Ann. Paul.*, p. 255; *Flores*, iii. 331; Trokelowe, p. 64.
[22] Below, App. I. 3.   [23] *Ann. Paul.*, p. 262; *Vita*, p. 30. Compare 2 Sam. 1: 26.

APPENDIX I

Westminster Abbey and Gaveston in 1308 and 1309

1. LETTER written from Avignon by Roger de Aldenham to Reginald de Hadham, prior, and to Henry de Bircheston, Guy de Ashwell, and Philip de Sutton, monks of Westminster (WAM 5460 (parchment roll of the first quarter of the fourteenth century), m. 1, lines 1–55). The letter was written after the king's assent to Kedyngton's election as abbot (23 February 1308) and perhaps after Hadham's reinstatment as prior on 17 May (Pearce, *Walter de Wenlok*, p. 193), but before Gaveston and John Charlton left for Ireland in late June. Two of the schedules which were apparently attached to the letter are printed below as 1.a and 1.b. See above, ch. 3.

Eandem quam sibi graciam et salutem. Videtis et scitis, domini et fratres mei dilectissimi, quod ab inicio contencionis jam diu inter nos pro statu monasterii nostri communi ventilate[1] adversarii et emuli nostri se ipsos cum falsis cautelis, conjecturis, ymaginacionibus, per dolum adinventis litteris a potestatibus secularibus, ex omni parte munierunt et juvarunt et in multis contra Deum et justiciam hucusque preval[uerun]t. Ideo faciatis nunc demum secundum consilium vestrum in curia Romana et probemus[2] juvare nos ipsos et ecclesiam nostram cum cautelis veris[3] et per consilium nostrum ordinatis quas[4] scitis. Dominus rex primo noluit electum vestrum admittere nec secundo, ut michi electus ipse recognovit, et hoc propter vulgarem infamiam que in populo de ipso super multis criminibus et defectibus

---

[1] MS *ventilitate* corrected from *vtilitate*.   [2] *Sic* in MS.
[3] MS *veris* corrected from *vris*.   [4] MS *quia*.

laborabat. Quo viso idem electus, A. de Persor' et W. de Chalk' et Payn,[5] ad quorum manus mille libre sterlingorum de pecunia abbatis defuncti devenerunt, statim adheserunt domino Petro de Caveston' et, datis sibi C libris, ipse negocium electi et partis sue et fautorum suorum assumpsit erga quoscumque in utraque curia expediendum et finaliter per adjutorium et procuracionem suam ibi[6] terminandum. Sic enim idem Petrus causam abbatis defuncti contra conventum et statum ecclesie nostre assumpserat nuper promovendam. Et sic per istam viam electus habet omnes litteras quibuscumque voluerit impetrare. Unde consilium nostrum ordinavit unam viam valde cautam et fructuosam, que ultra modum nos potest juvare et litteras et informaciones factas pro electo totaliter adnulare, videlicet quod vos vel aliqui[7] vestrum caute, secrete et circumspecte procuretis comitissam Hereford' vel alios qui sunt familiares regine, ita quod ipsa comitissa vel aliquis vel aliqui istorum novam informent reginam caute et secrete de omnibus premissis, quomodo videlicet dictus dominus Petrus pro tanta pecunia[8] negocium abbatis defuncti et electi contra Deum et justiciam et statum ecclesie sue admisit fraudulenter et quomodo ipse Petrus de domino rege et aliis tot et tantas litteras pro dicto electo ad papam, regem Francie et ad cardinales procuravit ad preficiendum tanto monasterio hominem tam indignum pro pecunia sibi data ad confusionem et schandalum perpetuum capelle domini regis et tocius ordinis nostri. Et quod domina regina ita de omnibus hiis informetur quod propter odium illius Petri ipsa dignetur scribere specialiter et secrete[9] domino regi Francie, patri suo, pape, eciam cardinalibus et domino Karolo, fratri regis Francie, quod ipsi male sunt informati pro dicto electo contra Deum et justiciam per suggestionem et procuracionem predicti Petri maledicti factam domino regi. Et quod ipsa sub tali forma scribat patri suo, regi Francie, et Karolo, fratri suo, quod ipsi inpediant apud papam et cardinales illud negocium electi et fautorum suorum, quod dictus Petrus assumpsit sibi pro pecunia promovendum. Et dicit vestrum consilium in curia quod ista cautela, si ipsam ad effectum ducere potestis quoquomodo per amicos et bonas informaciones, omnia procurata pro electo in cinerem reducet. Ergo studeatis istud consilium et istam cautelam sequi et prosequi cum effectu erga dominam reginam provocatam[10] et salvi sumus ex omni parte. Dicit vero dominus meus[11] quod nollet pro magna pecunia quod non habuisset litteras quas pro me impetrastis de eadem regina ad papam et dominum Reymundum de Gout'.[12]

---

[5] For Brothers Alexander de Persore, William de Chalk, and Henry Payn, see Pearce, *The Monks of Westminster*, pp. 62, 66, 71.   [6] MS *vbi*.   [7] -li- interlined.
[8] *pecunia* interlined.   [9] *et secrete* interlined.   [10] *provocatam* interlined.
[11] This is a reference to Thomas Jorz, cardinal priest of S. Sabina, the 'English cardinal'.
[12] Raymond de Got, nephew of Clement V, was cardinal deacon of S. Maria Nova.

Dominus meus ipsemet ipsas litteras recepit et portavit, et multum juvant ad informacionem quam dominus meus prius[13] fecerat eisdem, quia ex hiis intelligitur quod mirabiliter et diversimode per procuraciones emanaverant tales littere. Et ideo dominus consulit quod circa istam cautelam faciendam totis viribus insistatis per omnem viam quam excogitare potestis ut optatum[14] nostrum habere possimus secundum veritatem. Et vellet dominus quod consimiles litteras possetis procurare per easdem informaciones de comite Lyncoln', Hereford' et aliis comitibus quantumcumque potestis predicto regi Francie, pape et cardinalibus, quia tempus habetis congruum et acceptabile ad procurandum litteras et alia contra omnes quos fovebat ipse Petrus, nec de regina nec de comitibus, si bene informentur super hiis que predixi, repulsam habebitis aliquam, quia quicquid ipsum Petrum vel suos tangit quoquomodo et regina et comites, papa eciam et cardinales et rex eciam Francie desiderant et leti erunt inpedire. Ergo vigiletis et agatis quod potestis viriliter circa istam cautelam et tristicia vestra vertetur in gaudium. Et si tales litteras potestis impetrare per aliquam viam, eas michi celeriter per latorem presencium transmittatis cum copiis ipsarum litterarum, ut dominus meus de contentis ante presentacionem ipsarum litterarum possit informar[i], et studeatis et procuretis quod ipse littere sint graciose et bene concepte, ita quod rogetur dominus rex Francie et papa pro aliquo promovendo qui sit utilis et sufficiens pro ecclesia et nominetis illum quem talem reputatis, priorem vel Henricum vel Gwydonem vel Philippum.[15] Ista omnia emanarunt de magno tractatu et consilio dominorum. Ergo non dormiatis, quia dominus meus et nos vigilamus. Credo quod dominus Johannes de Ferar' et dominus Robertus de Tauney sint amici vestri, set nescio utrum teneant cum domino Petro vel non; si non, tunc possent expedire vos et procurare hujusmodi litteras de comitibus Lync', Warewyk' et Hereford'. Et si[16] de hiis omnibus litteras habere non potestis, summopere de comite Lyncoln', qui major est omnium et cui papa, cardinales et rex Francie plus credunt et diligunt inpetretis. Frater Philippus et Gwydo fingant se ire per maner[ia] ad spaciandum, quia sic possunt sine suspicione ire ad comites ubicumque fuerint et hujusmodi litteras per amicos procurare; et hoc celeriter faciant pro Jhesu Cristo et vos, domine prior, interim procuretis episcopum London' quod scribat domino meo Anglico cardinali et testificet famam et conversacionem electi, angustias et veritates vestras et statum meum in omnibus et quomodo ivi ad curiam, quia dominus meus multum diligit episcopum et credit ei tanquam viro probo et perfecto.

---

[13] *prius* interlined.   [14] MS *optentum*.

[15] This is a reference to the writer's four correspondents, Reginald de Hadham, Henry de Bircheston, Guy de Ashwell, and Philip de Sutton.   [16] *si* interlined.

Penitet[17] ultra modum quod tu, frater Gwydo, ita insipienter renunciasti
juri tuo, verumtamen quicquid[18] inter vos factum fuit ipso die de prima,
secunda et tercia eleccione viciosum et ruinosum fuit ipso jure. Hoc dicit
totum consilium, quia indiscrete, precipitanter et extra omnem formam
debitam totum factum est, unde doleo quod in tam solempni facto non fuit
inter tot capita aliqua sapiencia vel circumspeccio. Mittatis michi quare
Jordanus noluit michi inter alios aliquid dare de residuo distribucionis.
Rogetis Ranulphum[19] quod michi aliquid det de camera vel saltem de gracia
sua; jam potest videre quod sum absolutus a sentencia abbatis, que tamen
nulla fuit, quicquid dicat Thomas de Wenlok' vel alii adversarii nostri ad
scaccarium vel alibi de persona mea, totum mentiti sunt, et hoc paratus sum
probare per dominum meum et alios de curia fidedignos, quia non [est][20]
homo vivens in terra qui unquam de ore meo quicquam audivit pronunciari
de domino rege vel suis ministris clam vel palam, absit a me, nec me oppono
contra electum in aliquo, teneo me clausum; alios tamen a prosecucione juris
sui non possum repellere nec debeo. Istud dicatis confidenter, non me
intromitto de electo nec de opponentibus, quia dominus meus non
permitteret, licet vellem.

Istas litteras, quia magne sunt efficacie et utilitatis, legatis inter vos
quatuor, januis[21] super vos clausis, cum deliberacione ter vel quater, ut
tenorem totum intelligatis; legat unus et alii audiant et intelligant unam
cedulam post aliam per ordinem; non rapiat unusquisque cedulam et legat
per se sicut soliti estis; novi bene modum vestrum et ideo hoc dico.

Priori, Henrico, Gwydoni et Philippo, per R. de Aldenham.

1a. Schedule 1 to Aldenham's letter (WAM 5460, m. 1, lines 82–117)

Secunda. Consilium eciam vestrum ordinavit quod, si comes Lync' sit in
aliquo loco juxta London' ad unam dietam vel duas, quod vos, domine prior,
cum socio vel duobus ipsum comitem adeatis, assumpto vobiscum magistro
Johanne de Deneby vel aliquo alio clerico circumspecto, cadatis proni in
terram ante eum in camera sua vel genibus flexis interpelletis eum humiliter
verbis et vocibus lacrimosis quod ipse pro pietate Dei, pro reverencia et
honore beatorum Petri et Edwardi, patronorum vestrorum, vobis afflictis et
ecclesie vestre desolate ac oppresse misericordie sue viscera pro salute
animarum progenitorum suorum dignetur clementer aperire et vobis contra
oppressores vestros suum patrocinium exhibere, ipsum attencius flagitando

---

[17] The word *penitet* is preceded by a sign indicating that the passage which follows should be
inserted elsewhere.   [18] MS *quicquis.*
[19] For Jordan [de Wratting] and Ranulph [de Salop], see Pearce, *The Monks of Westminster,*
pp. 55, 76.   [20] [*est*] is not in MS.   [21] MS ? *janinis.*

quod oppressiones et gravamina ecclesie sibi possitis exponere viva voce, incipientes quomodo abbas jam defunctus elemosinas domini regis et totum statum monasterii ita destruxerat et oppresserat quod necessario vos oportuit remedium querere aliunde. Et viso quod erga ipsum pro statu ecclesie jus vestrum prosequi voluistis, idem abbas, advertens quod, si opera sua in palam devenissent, quod confusus fuisset ipso jure, statim adhesit domino Petro de Gaveston', et datis sibi CC libris sterlingorum et aliis exenniis infinitis, idem Petrus defensionem abbatis contra vos statim assumpsit et dominum regem qui nunc est contra vos in tantum provocavit et excitavit quod audienciam super injuriis et oppressionibus vobis illatis numquam habere potuistis et sic ipsum abbatem usque ad mortem fovebat et defendebat contra Deum et veritatem, volens preterea nobis gravissimam penam et quibusdam exilium decrevisse et decrevit. Tandem mortuo abbate accidit quod fautores ipsius abbatis per conspiracionem, collusionem et juramentum inter ipsos per viam confederacionis prestitura quod ipsi fautores sic confederati vobis prevaluerunt in eleccione et quemdam de suis complicibus illiteratum, irreligiosum, in omnibus insufficientem, diversis criminibus et infamiis fornicacionis et adulterii irretitum ipsis similem elegerunt, quem dominus rex propter vulgarem infamiam de ipso electo in populo laborantem semel et secundo admittere recusavit; quo viso ipse electus et fautores sui dicto Petro iterato adheserunt et, datis sibi C libris de pecunia abbatis defuncti, idem Petrus expedicionem ipsius electi assumpsit erga quoscumque in utraque curia finaliter promovendam et expediendam, et sic procuravit ipsum admitti a rege et litteras ipsius regis et regine ad papam, cardinales et ad regem Francie pro dicto electo ad confusionem ecclesie expediendo procuravit. Et quod ipse dominus rex et thesaurarius ad procuracionem et instanciam dicti Petri et Johannis de Cherleton', secretarii sui, non desistunt litteras suas ad curiam Romanam et ad regem Francie indies multiplicare, unde per informacionem ipsarum litterarum dominus rex Francie scripsit domino pape et cardinalibus pro dicto electo expediendo. Set dominus rex Francie ignorat de infamia et insufficiencia electi et de procuracione ipsius Petri, quod si sciret, totaliter ipsum impediret. Unde supplicando rogetis dictum comitem quod pro Dei misericordia vos et ecclesiam dignetur sub suo patrocinio collocare et vos et monasterium contra informacionem ipsius Petri et Johannis in instanti necessitate adjuvare, ne tanto monasterio tamque[22] famoso talis diffamatus et indignus preficiatur ad confusionem ordinis et ecclesie scandalum et oppressionem, ita quod idem comes sic de premissis omnibus et aliis meliori modo quo scitis et potestis informatus dignetur scribere domino pape et duobus cardinalibus, Reymundo

---

[22] MS *tamquam.*

videlicet[23] et domino meo, regi eciam Francie et domino Carolo quod ipsi, per litteras suas de veritate vestra et falsa procuracione ipsius Petri plenius informati, expedicionem electi tam indigni impediant et provideant de idoneo per vos eidem comiti, si expedit, nominando, et obligetis vos et ecclesiam vestram eidem comiti imperpetuum, ut ipse cicius cordi habeat quod rogatis.

Non[24] timeas adire comitem, quoniam pro certo propter odium ipsius Petri vos juvabit cum effectu, et per ipsum et reginam omnes alii, papa videlicet, cardinales, rex Francie et dominus Carolus, si sint bene informati, idem facient cum favore, quoniam tamquam viro probo et perfecciori de regno ipsius comit[i] credunt et preterea Petrum ad mortem odio habent. Istud idem erga reginam secrecius studeatis procurare, quoniam, si ista facere possitis, salvi sumus omnes imperpetuum et eciam ecclesia[25] ad statum debitum per hoc erit reformata. Probetis ex omni parte quomodo per vos et amicos vestros poteritis ista procurare et hoc cum omni festinacione qua potestis. Sciatis quod electus habet sufficienter ad expendendum per manus J. de Butterl' et Curthygton'[26] et auditorum, nescio tamen quomodo, et nichilominus intendunt procurare regem et thesaurarium quod vos compellant ad obligandum monasterium ulterius pro electo et hoc nullo modo faciatis; cicius carcerem intretis.

Omnia[27] ista et alia quecumque vos gravant et comitem movere possunt ad pietatem eidem declaretis. Potest per hoc habere materiam regem Anglie et consilium suum melius informandi in tempore et nunc est tempus omnia ista suggerendi. Ideo vigiletis dum tempus oportunum habetis. Fingatis aliquam certam causam quando prior vadit ad comitem, ut nullus percipiat circa que laboratis; non dicatis nec garcioni nec capellano causam itineris vestri.

Priori, Henrico, Guidoni, Philippo.

1b. Schedule 2 to Aldenham's letter (WAM 5460, m. 1, lines 118–20; m. 2, lines 1–21).

Ista cedula deberet fuisse cum duabus cedulis simul ligatis cum filo interius. Ideo istam cum ipsis legatis in fine.

Et dicatis et exponatis similiter dicto comiti quomodo ad procuracionem electi et instanciam dicti Petri fratres vestri fuerunt per tantum tempus incarcerati et aliis omnibus sub certa pena fuit inhibitum ne aliquis contra

---

[23] This is another reference to Raymond de Got, cardinal deacon of S. Maria Nova.
[24] This word is preceded by a paragraph mark.   [25] *ecclesia* interlined.
[26] For John de Butterle and (?) William de Curtlington, see Pearce, *The Monks of Westminster*, pp. 67, 74.   [27] This word is preceded by a paragraph mark.

electum juste vel injuste, clam vel palam prosequeretur jus ecclesie, et
quomodo intendunt procurare vel procurarunt litteras regi Francie ut
caperet me[28] Rogerum et omnia alia gravamina, vobis et ecclesie per
procuracionem ipsius Petri illata, que excogitare potestis eidem intimetis,
quomodo diffamati et tantis sceleribus irretiti, qui ordinem vestrum
diffamarunt, eis consimilem elegerunt, qui ipsos in suis sceleribus et
inmundiciis foverunt sicut abbas jam defunctus, et quomodo vos compellunt
vel compellere intendunt obligare et confundere ecclesiam vestram pro dicto
misero electo et totum per corrupcionem munerum datorum dicto Petro,
Johanni de Cherleton' et aliis qui sic dominum regem informant omni die.
Sciatis quod hujusmodi informacio de premissis non solum ad unum valet,
set ad plura in futurum que modo non videtis. Videatis eciam et probetis si
per aliquos amicos possetis facere suggestionem domine regine et comiti
Linc' contra dominum Johannem de Cherleton', camerarium, secretarium
predicti Petri ab inicio, qui diu noctuque non cessat nobis malum procurare
per instinctum nequissimi carettarii,[29] nepotis sui, qui est inter vos, quoniam
iste dominus Johannes multa mala nobis fecit et non desistit; si scirent regina
et comes Linc' qualis est ipse, aliqualiter ipsum a potestate sua deponerent et
amoverent. Utinam[30] scirent quid dictum est de eo, quia, dum ipse stat in
tanta potestate, qu[an]to in ipso est, nos et ecclesiam semper infestabit.
Sciatis pro certo quod dominus meus dominum regem Francie de hiis et aliis
ad plenum vult informare et contra partem adversam excitare et ideo vellet
dominus quod ad confirmandum omnia verba sua que intendit dicere dicto[31]
regi, quod vos ex habundanti litteras prelocutas possetis de regina et comite
scilicet[32] Linc' celeriter impetrare, [*Francie rex*][33] majorem fidem adhereret
dictis domini mei et forsitan cum ipso domino meo iret ad papam et rogaret
pro nostro nominato pro quo decreveritis quod regina et comes in litteris suis
rogarent. De litteris vestris, laboribus, diligencia et expensis et diversis
infinitis beneficiis vobis omnibus assurgo ad graciarum acciones, et penitet
me et erubesco vehementer quod tociens et in tantis me oportuit vos vexare,
quod de vestra inpotencia, inopia et angustia cotidiana satis novi, set arta
necessitas[34] ad vos vexandum me compellit. Remaneat domi frater J. de
Lond'; nolo quod periculum incurrat et regraciamini sibi de bono proposito.
Agatis ita caute in omnibus que continentur in hiis litteris quod nullus in
mundo de hiis sciat nisi vos quatuor intitulati exterius. De curialitate et

---

[28] MS *me* (*et* interlined) *Rogerum*. The addition of *et* is clearly an error attributable to the
copyist, since the writer of the letter is without doubt Roger de Aldenham.
[29] Corrected in MS from *cartarii*.   [30] Corrected in MS from *Ut nam*.
[31] MS *domino*.   [32] MS ? *sl'm*.   [33] MS ? *et uter .n.*
[34] MS *necessitat'*.

expensis factis nunciis et procurator[i] domini mei, idem dominus est ita placatus et contentus quod mirum est dicere, et hoc bene monstrat in opere cum in ultimo posse suo sero et mane,[35] quia nunquam habuit aliquod negocium ita cordi sicut vestrum et hoc sepius dixit pluribus. Sequamini ergo consilium et doctrinam suam pro posse vestro et habebitis victoriam; licet dominus rex noster sit modo motus et excitatus contra nos, tamen scio et spero quod, postquam dominus rex Francie et dominus Carolus fuerint[36] per litteras regine et comitis melius informati, cito et leviter nostrum regem nobis facient per litteras suas placatum, quas litteras spero habere per dominum meum, si vos in aliis premissis possetis expediri.

Priori, Henrico de Bercheston', Gwydoni et Philippo.

2. Reginald de Hadham, prior of Westminster, to Master Walter Islip, royal treasurer in Ireland (WAM 5460, m. 1d, lines 66–73; June 1308–June 1309; probably spring 1309).

Discreto viro et amico suo karissimo magistro Waltero de Istelep', illustris regis Anglie in Hybernia thesaurario, frater Reginaldus de Hadham, prior Westm', salutem in omnium salvatore. Quia intelleximus quod dilectus nobis in Cristo Rogerus de Aldenham, confrater noster, ad aliquorum emulorum instigacionem, quibus semper gravis est vita bonorum, apud dominum regem et aliquos magnates exstitit nequiter accusatus eciam sine causa, vestram amiciciam in qua confidentissimam gerimus fiduciam una cum fidedignis fratribus quorum Deus tetigit corda attencius requirimus et rogamus quatinus Dei amore nostrique contemplacione instare velitis erga dominum Petrum de Gavaston' et ab ipso impetrare litteras deprecatorias erga dominum regem ut predicto fratri Rogero omnem rancoris sui offensam dignetur clementer remittere ejus precibus et amore. Speramus equidem vos pro hoc negocio a Domino mercedem consequi eternam, et nos et ecclesiam nostram[37] in posterum vestris beneplacitis et honori cum affectu astringimus et benivolo animo obligamus. Que autem feceritis circa premissa nobis vestris per proximum intervenientem dignemini intimare. Valete semper prospere in filio virginis gloriose ut optamus nos valere.

[35] Apparently *sic* in MS.   [36] MS *fuerant*.   [37] *nostram* interlined.

3. [Roger de Aldenham] to Ralph [de Mordon], Guy [de Ashwell] and other supporters in the convent of Westminster (WAM 5460, m. 1d (line 74)–m. 2d (last line); Avignon, Trinity Sunday, [25 May 1309]).

Cordibus suis salutem et seipsum. Regracior vobis, fratres mei dilectissimi, de infinitis vestris beneficiis michi ab antiquo et maxime in meis angustiis factis similiter atque procuratis. Frater Radulfe, rogo vos quod inter vos et Gwydonem unum beneficium michi faciatis in eventu videlicet quod, quia novi quod, quamcito venerit dominus P. de C.[38] ad Angliam, statim emuli mei ad ipsum ibunt vel specialem nuncium destinabunt et sibi legent litteras quas contra me fabricarunt, quas dicunt se de manu mea invenisse, et excitabunt eum contra me ut ipse inducat regem forsan ad scribendum contra me ad curiam, unde quia dominus Johannes de Cant' capellanus domini Johannis de Brittannia, amicus tuus et specialis fidelissimus,[39] michi dixit quod dominus Petrus de C. ultra modum diligit dominum suum Johannem antedictum et in litteris suis vocat eum patrem et ipse econverso filium, eo quod idem dominus P. de C. vult facere et procurare quod eum[40] rogaverit dominus Johannes, quod vos cum aliis amicis vestris, quamcito intellexeritis adventum domini Petri, sic instetis per dominum Robertum de Hausted' et alios amicos vestros erga dictum dominum Johannem quod ipse mutet voluntatem P. et a parte nobis contraria avertat animum suum et quod per vestras informaciones sibi datas informet dictum dominum Petrum de gestu fratris W.[41] et fautorum suorum et fama illorum et quomodo discurrunt hincinde sicut vagi et profugi sine licencia superioris, nunc ad regem, nunc ad scaccarium, nunc ad Ingelard', nunc ad justiciarios et alios regales, faciendo falsas suggestiones, perversas procuraciones, fabricando falsas litteras, ipsas michi et aliis imponendo, excitando brigas contra priorem et alios bonos viros, per quod perit religio, ordo negligitur, cultus divinus diminuitur, caritas extinguitur, oracionum suffragia in defraudacionem nostrorum fundatorum subtrahuntur, bona monasterii dissipantur et distrahuntur, ecclesia ruit et destruitur. Si vero dictus dominus Johannes de istis racionibus et motivis fuerit ad plenum per vos·instructus et

---

[38] *P. de C.*, i.e. Piers Gaveston, whose name in Westminster documents is sometimes given as *Petrus de Causton'* or *Caveston'*. See Harvey, *Wenlok*, pp. 120, 201; above, App. I. 1.

[39] On 18 Aug. 1310 John of Canterbury (*de Cantuaria*) was granted a protection with clause 'volumus' for one year for going to Gascony with the earl of Richmond (*CPR 1307–1313*, p. 277).   [40] MS *cum*.

[41] Probably William de Chalk, a supporter of Kedyngton (Pearce, *The Monks of Westminster*, p. 66).

ipsa domino Petro bono modo exposuerit, animum dicti domini Petri a nostris emulis totaliter et contra ipsos mutare poterit pro certo et similiter excitare. Nam de ipso plus confidunt,[42] si venerit; et ipse ignorat illorum falsitates, et dicitur quod homo est bone consciencie dominus Petrus, quando videt veritatem. Et [si][43] sciret et audiret premissa ab ore domini Johannis, non audiret de cetero aliquem de emulis nostris, qui nunquam cessabunt discurrere et procurare contra nos et nostros quamdiu sic audiuntur et foventur a predictis regalibus et donec repulsam et redarguicionem habeant ab aliquo tali magnate in quo precipue confidebant. Et inducatur dominus Petrus quod dicat illis, cum ad eum venerint, quod de cetero non confidant de ipso nec ad eum veniant pro talibus sicut prius, et quod dicat ipsis verba aspera et quod remaneant in claustro sicut status eorum requirit, ne deterius eis contingat. Frater Gwido, scripsi tibi nuper in alia littera quod dictum erat communiter in curia quod dominus Reymundus assumpserat negocium electi expediendum. Postea audivi ab ore unius cardinalis quod non[44] erat verum nec erit. Unde spero quod prioratus de Burley[45] non vacabit in curia sicut sperabat Paganus et ille cum capite transverso sagebers microcosmi.[46] Rogo ergo quod viriliter, caute et secrete insistatis in predicto negocio, quod si expediatur, salubre erit pro me et pro vobis in eternum. Et si non venerit dominus Petrus vel licet venerit, bonum esset, eciam peroptimum, quod premissas raciones et motivas exponeret idem dominus Johannes domino regi, asserendo eidem regi quod maximum peccatum est tales homines sic diffamatos in suis maliciis exaudire et fovere. Istam litteram non perdatis in medio claustri sicut facit prior noster. Dat' Avynion' die sancte Trinitatis.

---

[42] Followed by *si*, partly erased at the end of the line.   [43] *si* omitted in MS.

[44] *non* interlined.

[45] This is probably an error for *Hurley*, as kindly suggested by Miss Barbara Harvey.

[46] *Paganus* is undoubtedly Henry Payn; *ille cum capite transverso* may be a cryptic reference to Alexander de Persore, based on dubious etymology; the word *sagebers*, probably the French version of the Latin *sagibaro*, may be a further cryptic reference to another supporter of Kedyngton, Th. de Segesber', who seems to have been one of the abbot-elect's proctors in Avignon (Pearce, *The Monks of Westminster*, pp. 62, 71, 73). The word *microcosmi* may be a misreading of one or more words which were meant to refer, once again cryptically, to William de Chalk; one of these words may have been *cretosus* (chalky).

The Newcastle Jewels

Great seal letters patent in which Edward II acknowledges receipt of the jewels, horses, and other goods seized in Newcastle-upon-Tyne and elsewhere 'by reason of Piers Gaveston' (PRO C 66/138, m. 3 (originally a separate roll of one membrane, stitched on to the Patent Roll): *Foedera*: R. II. i. 203–5; Windsor, 27 February 1313).

Endorsed: Rotulus de restitucione jocalium et equorum captorum apud Novum Castrum super Tynam.

Edward par la grace de Dieu roi Dengleterre, seignur Dirlande et ducs Daquitaine, a touz ceux qe cestes lettres verront ou orrunt, salutz. Sachez nous avoir resceu par les meins del honurable piere en Dieu Wautier evesque de Wirecestr' et Johan de Sandale, liu tenaunz de noz chaunceler e tresorer, par nostre mandement et en nostre noun recevaunz de Thomas counte de Lancastre, Guy counte de Warrewik', Henri de Percy et Robert de Clifford' par les meyns Humfrei de Bohun counte de Hereford' et de Essex', e le dit Robert de Clifford' et Johan Buteturte deliveraunz les joiaus, chevaux e les autres choses desuz escrites, cest asavoir:

[1] Un hanap' dargent dorre enamaille sur un trepir ove covercle enamaille e les armes Dengleterre e de Fraunce en le pee, qi poisent sis livres dis et oit souz quatre deniers, e vaut quatre foiz le pois.

[2] Item quinze fermaux dor de divers pris, cest asavoir un qi poise sis souz oit deners, pris de vint mars.

[3] Item un fermaille qe poisse quatorze deniers.

[4] Item un autre fermaille qe poise quatre souz quatre deniers, pris de vint livres.

[5] Item un autre fermaille qe peise quatre souz dis deners, pris de vint livres.

[6] Item un autre fermaille qe poise deux souz sept deners, pris de quarrant' souz.

[7] Item un autre fermaille qe peise treis souz un dener, pris de dis livres.

[8] Item un autre fermaille qe poise neof' deniers maille ferling.

[9] Item un autre fermaille qe poise deux souz dis deners ferling.

[10] Item un autre fermaille qe poise trezze soutz, pris de trente livres.

[11] Item un autre fermaille qe poise sis deners, pris de sept souz sis deners.

[12] Item un autre fermaille qe poisse dis deners, pris de dozze souz sis deners.

[13] Item un autre fermaille qe poise vint treis deners ferling.

[14] Item un autre fermaille, pris de deus souz.

[15] Item un autre fermaille qe poisse deux deners, pris de deus souz sis deners.

[16] Item un autre fermaille qe poise deux deners.

[17] Item en un autre clutet dozze fermaux dor, cest asaver une nouche dor ove un camaeu blank'.

[18] Item un fermaille dor qe poise quatre deners e done au roy qe ore est par sire Johan de Leek'.

[19] Item un autre fermaille done au roi par madame Isabelle, la seor, qe poise oit deners.

[20] Item un autre fermaille du doun Edmon counte de Cornewaile a madame Isabelle, la seor, qe poise quatre deners.

[21] Item un autre fermail' done au roi as bones estreines lan vint e secund a Langele.

[22] Item un autre fermaille du doun madame la roine.

[23] Item un autre fermaille du doun la reine.

[24] Item un autre fermaille du doun madame la roine, la miere.

[25] Item quatre fermeaux sanz bille e nient prisez od perie.

[26] Item un autre fermail dor enamaille sanz bille et nient prise.

[27] Item en un autre clutet trois fermeaux dor, cest asavoir un qe poise sept deners, done par la duchesse de Brabant.

[28] Item un autre fermaille du doun le prior del Hospital, qe poise cink' deners.

[29] Item un autre fermaille nient prise ne poise et un anel done a sire Anfons[1] par sire Williame de Salines.

[30] Item une nouche dor od deux amiraudes, deux rubiz, deux saphirs e unze margeries, od un camaeu en miliu, qe poise cink' souz sis deners maille, del devis la reigne Dalemaigne.

[31] Item un joial dor od neof' amiraudes e neof' gernettes, od un camaeu blank' en milieu, enamaille dautre part, nient prise ne poisse.

---

[1] MS *Anfour*. Probably Alfonso, son of Edward I (born 24 Nov. 1273; died Aug. 1284).

[32] Item un fermaille dor od deux admiraudes, deux rubiz, quatre margeries et un saphir en milieu, pris de cent sessant livres de turneis.

[33] Item une nouche dor de diverse perie, pris de cent livres de turneis.

[34] Item une nouche dor od quatre amiraudes, cink rubiz, quatre margeries, pris de sis vint livres de turneis.

[35] Item une nouche dor de diverse perie, pris de cinquant livres de turneis.

[36] Item un autre tiele nouche dor, pris aussint de cinquant livres de turneis.

[37] Item une nouche dor de viel overaigne, qe poise deux souz sis deners maille.

[38] Item un joial dor od petites amiraudes, od un camaeu neir en milieu, resceu del evesqe de Baa et de Welles.

[39] Item une croice dor od deux rubiz baleis, trois saphirs, quatre margeries, qe poisent trois souz neof' deners, pris de quatre mars.

[40] Item en mesme lescrene² sept rubiz gros et un rubi baleis, deux petiz rubitz, dis petites amiraudes en aneaux dor desoutz³ un baston.

[41] Item une grosse gernette e un saphir petit sur mesme le baston, les queles sont du viel tresor le roi, sicome piert par une bille pendaunte par mesme le bastoun.

[42] Item un grant anel au feur de pontifical od quatre baleis.

[43] Item sis rubiz en aneaux sur un autre bastoun, de mesme le tresor.

[44] Item sur un autre baston trois rubiz, un amiraude, un peridot, un topas,⁴ de mesme le tresor.

[45] Item sur un autre baston deux rubiz, deux saphirs, un gernette, un cristal, dount les cink' furent liverez par executours des evesqes e le sisme par la fille Leulyn prince de Gales, bilettez e prisez touz a dis mars.

[46] Item sur un autre baston cink' rubiz beaux, qe sont prisez a cessant trois livres, sicome piert par les billes.

[47] Item sur un autre bastoun deux saphirs, dount lun fust a lesveque de Baa e lautre al . . abbe de Abbyndon'.

[48] Item sur un autre baston oit diamanz, dont les cink' sont grant e les trois petiz.

[49] Item sur un autre baston oit amiraudes, dount lune fust done par Thomas ercevesque Deverwik'.

[50] Item sur un autre baston sept aneux faitz au feur des seaus, du viel tresor.

[51] Item sur un autre bastoun dis diamanz, de mesme le tresor.

[52] Item sur un autre bastoun deux rubiz, cink' saphirs, un diamant, un

---

² MS *lestrene*.   ³ *desoutz* interlined.   ⁴ MS *tepas*.

camaeu, qe furent donez par divers esvesqes e abbez, de mesme le tresor, sicome piert par les billes.

[53] Item sur un autre bastoun quatre rubiz, un anel gemmeu od un rubi, une amiraude, un baleis e un diamant, de mesme le tresor.

[54] Item sur un autre bastoun un saphir cressant od une esteille feite des amiraudes dedeinz.

[55] Item un anel od un rubi e un autre anel od une amiraude e un rubi.

[56] Item en un petit[5] drapelet diverses pieres de divers colours, qe furent resceuz par la mayn sire Hughe de Notingham de levesque de Baa, de viele tresor, lan [vintisme][6] quinte.

[57] Item un anel dor od un saphir, le quel seint Dunstan forga de ses mayns.

[58] Item un amatistre en or e un saphir e un barel dor ove reliques.

[59] Item sept pieres enchastonez, dount nous ne savoms les nons forqe jaspre e amatistre.

[60] Item un camaeu en or de Israel.

[61] Item deux diamanz, deux amiraudes, un camaeu en anel dor e dedeinz une boiste dargent enamaile.

[62] Item une boiste dargent endorre pur porter eynz un anel entour le col de un homme.

[63] Item une croiz dor ove diverses pieres, un tache dor ove diverse pieres, deux aneaux a feur de seaux.

[64] Item un pot dargent od diverses pieres.

[65] Item sur un autre baston deux saphirs, dount lune fust al evesque Gilbert de Cicestr'.

[66] Item un cofin garni dargent endorre, en quel les susdites choses furent, sauve la coupe.

[67] Item une grant rubi hors dor, qe fust trove sur sire Piers[7] de Gavaston' quant il fust pris, le pris de mille livres.

[68] Item un rubi en un anel dor, qe est apele la cerise, qe fust au roi.

[69] Item trois grantz rubiz en aneaus, une amiraude, un diamaund de grant pris, en une boiste dargent enamaille, qe fust trove sur le dit Pieres quant il fust pris.

[70] Item deux perides, lun en argent, lautre en or.

[71] Item deux seaux, un grant e un petit, e au petit seal une clief' pendaunte, un esterling' plie et un calcedoyne, les queux furent trovez en sa burse quant il fuit pris.

[72] Item en un cofre lie de feer une mirour dargent enamaille, un pigne, un priket, qe fust done au roi par la contesse de Bare a Gant.

---

[5] *petit* interlined.   [6] *vintisme* omitted in MS.   [7] *Piers* interlined.

[73] Item une peire des coteaux enamaille, qe furent done au roi par la duchesse de Brabant.

[74] Item un autre peire de coteaux enamaille.

[75] Item un grant pot pur amoigne dargent nient prise.

[76] Item quatre barils de ivoir garniz de latoun od les coffines.

[77] Item en un [au]tre coffre un ceint[ure][8] dargent od eschuchons barrez dargent enamaille, qe poise quatre livres dis souz.

[78] Item une autre ceinture de soie coverte des perles, pris de dis livres.

[79] Item dis pieces dorfreis de tars, deux dras de tars vermeaux diasprez.

[80] Item une cote armere des armes sire Pieres.

[81] Item une autre ceinture de quir de lioun harnesse dor od camaeux, pris de cent sessant sis livres tresze souz quatre deners.

[82] Item un dragon dorre od les eles enamaile, qe poise sessant et cink' souz dis deners od le cofin de quir.

[83] Item une coupe dor od le covercle, qe peise sessant' un souz oite deners.

[84] Item un hanap dor od le covercle dorre enamaile sur un trepir dorre, qe poise cinquant' neof' souz deux deners.[9]

[85] Item une coupe dor od le covercle dor, qe poise quaraunt souz dis deners od un touche pur assaer or.

[86] Item deux godetz dor, dount lun ad covercle, qe poise trent' souz, e lautre sanz covercle, qe poise cink' souz dis deners, od deux coffins de quir.

[87] Item une coupe dor enamaille od perie, que la reigne Alianore devisa au roi qi ore est od sa beniceon, qe poise cessant dis et oit souz quatre deners.

[88] Item un saler dor, qe poise dis e sept souz dis deners, od un forel dargent dedentz, qe poise quatre souz sept deners.

[89] Item un hanap' dor plein sanz pee od le covercle dor, qe poise vint sis souz oit deners.

[90] Item une coupe dor, qe poise cinkaunte deux souz sis deners.

[91] Item duze quillers dor, qe poisent vint un souz o une cas dargent, qe poise quinze souz quatre deners.

[92] Item un egle dor od rubiz, amiraudes, saphirs, margeries, od reliques dedenz de seint Richard de Cicestr' en un cas de quir.

[93] Item quinze quillers dor, qe poisent vint cink souz oit deners, od un cas dargent, qe poise unze souz, et un autre cas de quir pur mesmes ces.

[94] Item un coronal dor od diverse perie, pris de cent mars.

[95] Item un chapelet dargent de divers perie, pris de doze soutz.

[96] Item en un autre cofre un grant pot dargent od trois petz pur chaufer eawe, qe poise sis livres quinze soutz dis deners.

---

[8] MS *en untre coffre un ceint.*   [9] Entries 82–4 are interlined.

[97] Item une nef dargent endorre od qatre roefs, amaille par les costes, qe poise sept livres sesze soutz oyt deners.

[98] Item en un autre cofre un grant esquel dargent pur lamoine od un egle en le fonce derere, nient peise uncore, en un cas de quir lie de feer.

[99] Item en un autre cofre un pot dargent dorre enamaille, qe poise sis livres sis soutz oyt deners et vaut dis noef livres.

[100] Item un hanap dargent dorre od le covercle et od un pe bas et od un treper enamaille des armes Dengleterre et de Fraunce, e poisent le hanap e le covercle quaraunte sis souz oit deners, e le treper peise par sei sept souz, e vaut le dit hanap e le covercle e le treper trois foiz le pois.

[101] Item un pot dargent enamaille de mesmes les armes, qe poise cinquant' souz et vaut sept livres dis souz.

[102] Item une boiste divoyr hernise dargent od quatre peez.

[103] Item un hanap de cristal de veil tresor od le pee dargent od escochons, qe poise deux mars.

[104] Item deux salers dargent ove les covercles dargent, qe poisent quaraunt' souz.

[105] Item trois plates dargent por especierie, e poisent quatre livres.

[106] Item un hanap dargent saunz pee od le covercle dorre enamaille od un treper, qe poise cent dis souz dis deners, et vaut le treble pois.

[107] Item une coupe dargent dorre enamaille, qe poise quatre livres quinze souz, e vaut le treble pois.

[108] Item un pot dargent dorre enamaille pur ewe, qe poise cinquant' souz dis deners, e vaut duble pois e demy.

[109] Item une coupe dargent de viel tresor, qe fust al evesqe Gilbert de Cicestre, qe poise quarant' trois souz quatre deners.

[110] Item un autre coupe dargent blaunche, qe poise vint oit souz.

[111] Item un autre coupe dargent, qe poise trent' souz.

[112] Item un autre coupe dargent od le pomel enamaille des armes Dengleterre, qe poise quarant' sept soutz trois deners.

[113] Item une coupe dargent qe fust al ercevesque Henry Deverwik', qe poise quarant' sis souz oit deners, de veil tresor.

[114] Item un godet dargent pur ewe od sis godetz dedeinz e deux saliers od un covercle, qe peisent quatre livres sis souz.

[115] Item sis quillers dargent, qe poisent sept souz, dedeinz le cofyn od les godetz.

[116] Item un pot dargent, qe poise trente noef' soutz.

[117] Item un encenser dargent dorre, qe poise cinquante neof' souz.

[118] Item une neef' dargent pur encens, qe poise dis oit souz quatre deners.

[119] Item en un autre coffre en un escrene[10] un alver frette de perles qe fust done par la contesse de Flaundres au roi qe mort est a Gant.

[120] Item une ceynture hernisse divoir entaille od un aloer pendaunt, od un visage de Saracyn.

[121] Item une burse de drap' dor ove deux pierres de Jerusalem dedenz.

[122] Item en un autre coffre un pot dargent, qe poise quatre livres.

[123] Item un autre pot dargent, qe poise sessant sesze souz oit deners.

[124] Item un autre pot dargent, qe poise sesante ditz souz.

[125] Item un autre pot dargent, qe poisse sessant' unze souz unze deners.

[126] Item un autre pot dargent, qe poise sis livres dis oit souz quatre deners.

[127] Item un autre pot dargent, qe poise sessant cink' soutz.

[128] Item un autre pot dargent pur ewe, qe peise sessant' cink souz.

[129] Item une plate dargent od le pee por espicerie, qe poise quarant' souz.

[130] Item une peire de bascins dargent enamaile dedenz od escochons, qe poisent noef' livres cink' souz.

[131] Item un autre peire de bascins dargent dorrez, qe poisent sept livres tresze souz quatre deners.

[132] Item en un autre cofre sis bacins dargent od escochons des armes le dit Pieres en le fonce, qe poisent vint cink' livres.

[133] Item noef' chargeours dargent, qe poisent vint sis livres tresze souz quatre deners.

[134] Item deux plates dargent pur fruit des armes le roy Dengleterre, qe poisent sessant' dis oit souz quatre deners.

[135] Item cent esqueles dargent merchez dun egle, qe poisent cent vint et sis livres quinze souz deux deners.

[136] Item quaraunte oit saussers dargent de divers merches, qe peisent cesze livres cink' souz oit deners.

[137] Item en un autre coffre trent' sausers dargent, qe poisent noef' livres quinze souz.

[138] Item dis sept hanaps dargent merchiez del egle avauntdit, qe poisent unze livres cink souz oit deners.

[139] Item une peire des bascins dargent pur chapele, qe poisent quatre livres.

[140] Item vint hanaps dargent, qe poisent vint mars.

[141] Item trente sis quillers dargent, qe poisent quarant' sis souz oit deners, en un cas de quir.

<hr />

[10] MS *estrene.*

[142] Item un pot dargent pur ewe, qe poise cinquant cink' souz.

[143] Item une plate dargent debrise, qe poise vint sis souz.

[144] Item en un autre coffre un pot dargent, qe poise sis livres dis souz dis deners.

[145] Item un autre pot dargent, qe poise quatre livres tresze souz quatre deners.

[146] Item un autre pot dargent, qe poise quatre livres sesze souz oit deners.

[147] Item un autre pot dargent, qe poise sessant cink' souz.

[148] Item en un autre coffre un pot dargent pur ewe, qe peise quatre mars.

[149] Item un mors dargent od quatre botons dargent dorrez od deux lions pur chape de cuir.

[150] Item un remaneaunt de samit vert.

[151] Item un veil seal entaille e une perre de Calcedoine.

[152] Item trois chapelettes de petit pris.

[153] Item trois furchestes dargent pur mangier poires.

[154] Item une lange de serpent en argent.

[155] Item une ceinture de fil dargent blank'.

[156] Item une autre ceinture barre dargent et dorre, qe poise quarant trois souz.

[157] Item un autre petite ceinture de perles, pris de dis souz.

[158] Item un chapelet de Paris, pris de sis souz oit deners.

[159] Item une croice od une cheyne dargent, pris de quarant deners.

[160] Item une piere assise en or od une blaunche croice, croise de lui mesmes.

[161] Item une ceynture garnie dargent tissue de In principio.

[162] Item en un autre coffre un chesible simple, un chaliz dargent dorre, un tunicle,[11] un dalmaticle, deux aubes, une chape de quir de vaak,[12] un estole, deux fanons dune seute.

[163] Item un autre chesible, tunicle, dalmaticle, dosser, frontal de un drap de vert, poudre de oiseaus et de peissons dor.

[164] Item en un autre coffre une peire de plates enclouez et garniz dargent, od quatre cheynes dargent, coverz dun drap de velvet vermail besaunte dor.

[165] Item deux peires de jambers de feer veutz et noveaux.

[166] Item autres divers garnementz des armes le dit Pieres ovek' les alettes garniz et frettez de perles.

[11] Followed by an erasure.
[12] MS *Naak*. The medieval form of *cuir de vache* (cowhide) is wanted here.

[167] Item en un sak' un bacenet burny od surcils.

[168] Item un mantel de velvet raie furre de menevoir.

[169] Item vint cink pieces de draps de divers garnementz et de divers colours.

[170] Item en un autre saak' une peire de treppes des armes le dit Piers.

[171] Item un curtyn de cendal.

[172] Item deux cotes de velvet pur plates coverir.

[173] Item une houche pur palefrei des armes le roy.

[174] Item quatre chemises et trois brais de Gascoingne, orfresez.

[175] Item une veille banere des armes le dit Piers.

[176] Item en un autre coffre deux bascins dargent od les eschochons des armes sire Edmun[13] de Maulei, qe poisent sept livres quatre souz, od un hanaper lie de feer.

[177] Item une coupe dargent, qe poise vint sept souz.

[178] Item un pot dargent, qe poise cinquant' un souz deux deners.

[179] Item un autre coupe dargent od un pomel enamaille des armes de Fraunce et Dengleterre, qe poise quarant un souz deux deners.

[180] Item en un autre coffre deux lavours dargent, qe poisent quatre livres neof' souz sis deners, od deux cas de quir.

[181] Item deux potz dargent pur ewe, un dorre et lautre blank', qe poisent trente trois souz quatre deners, od deux cas de quir.

[182] Item une coupe dargent, qe poise vint sis souz oit deners.

[183] Item en un autre coffre trente esqueles dargent,[14] qe poisent vint oit livres quatre souz dis deners.

[184] Item trent cink' saussers dargent, qe poisent dis livres oit souz.

[185] Item vint un hanaps dargent, qe poisent dis livres vint deners.

[186] Item un pot dargent, qe poise cinquant' deux souz.

[187] Item une coupe dargent od un pomel enamaille des armes Dengleterre e de Fraunce, qe poise trent' trois souz quatre deners.

[188] Item dis oit quillers dargent, qe poisent dis oit souz.

[189] Item un saler dargent, qe poisze cesze souz.

[190] Item quarant un destres e coursers et un palefrei.

[191] Item noef' somers.

[192] Item duze chivaus charetters.

[193] Item deux charettes od tut le herneis.

Les queux choses avauntdites ensemblement od autres choses diverses qe ne sont pas especifiez en cestes noz lettres e sont contenues en une endenture de coe faite entre les ditz evesqe et Johan de Sandale, dune part pur nous et en noun de nous[15] recevaunz, et Johan de Herselarton', chivaler, e Michel de

---

[13] MS *Edmin.*   [14] *dargent* interlined.   [15] MS *noz* corrected to *nous.*

Meldon', en noun des avauntditz counte de Hereford', Robert de Clifford' et
Johan de Buteturte dautre part, estoient prises nadgerres par les avauntditz
counte de Lancastr' et de Warrewik', Henry et Robert a Noef' Chastel sur
Tyne et aillours par lenchesoun de Pieres de Gavaston'. De queux joiaux,
chivaus et totes autres choses en cestes lettres et en la dite endenture
contenues e par les avauntditz evesque et Johan de Sandale par suffisaunt
poair a eux par nous doneez resceues acquitoms et aquiteroms pur touz jours
par cestes noz lettres overtes [l]es avauntditz . . countes de Lancastr' et de
Warrewik', Henry et Robert et touz lur alliez et aerdaunz et mesnengs contre
totes gentz qi rien y porront demaunder. Et si leur busoigne daver autre
aquitaunce que ceste des choses rendues en cestes lettres et en la susdite
endenture contenues, si voloms qil leient solonc le tretiz de coe fait. Et auxi
voloms qe les choses nient restitues soient rendues ou le pris, ccst asavoir le
pris des chyvauz mortz e dautres chose gastez, perdues et nient restitues
entre cy et le mi quaresme, forspris joiaux, si nules seient arere, les queux
nous voloms qe soient al dit terme rendues et sur la livere eyent acquitaunce
solonc la forme de dit tretiz. En tesmoinance des queles choses nous
a[v]oms[16] fait faire cestes nos lettres overtes. Don' a Wyndes' le vint septime
jour de feverer.

[16] MS *aoms*.

INDEX

The following abbreviations have been used for French place-names: *arr.*: *arrondissement*; *cant.*: *canton*; *dép.*: *département*

Abingdon (Berks.), abbot of, sapphire of 127
Achilles 5, 8, 110
Adam, illegitimate son of Edward II 8
Æthelred II, king of England, sons of, *see* Alfred; Edward
Agenais (France), seneschal of, *see* Marsan, Arnaud Guillaume de
Airmyn, William, chancery clerk 80 n. 40
Albano, cardinal bishop of, *see* Aux, Arnaud d'
Albret, Amanieu d':
  letter of Edward II to 50
  objections of, to grants made in Guyenne to Gaveston and to Arnaud Guillaume de Marsan: appeals to Edward II 73; appeals to Philip IV 73; *see also* Nérac
Aldenham, Roger de, monk of Westminster, proctor in Avignon of the opponents of Richard de Kedyngton, the abbot elect:
  his candidates for the succession of Abbot Wenlok, *see* Ashwell, Guy de; Bircheston, Henry de; Hadham, Reginald de; Sutton, Philip de
  his fear of being arrested in France 62–3, 121
  his letters from Avignon to his friends in the abbey: (in 1308) 61–3, 115–22; (in 1309) 67–8, 114, 123–4
  his reference to Gaveston: in 1308 as 'the accursed Peter' 63, 116; in 1309 as a righteous man 67, 124
  in trouble with the king and the magnates 66, 123–4
  letters of support for, from Reginald de Hadham, *see* Islip, Walter
Alfonso, son of Edward I, brooch and ring given by William de Salines to 126
Alfred, son of Æthelred II, adoptive brother of Duke Robert I of Normandy 15
Almain, queen of, jewels bequeathed by 126
'Alney' (or 'Olney'), treaty between Cnut and Edmund Ironside concluded at 15–17, 112
Amiens (France, *dép.* Somme), letters patent under Henry III's great seal substitute dated at 38 n. 84

Anglo-Saxon Chronicle 15–16
annals and chronicles 7
  see also Anglo-Saxon Chronicle; Annals of Ireland; Annals of London; Annals of St Paul's; Baker; Bridlington; 'Chronicle of the Civil Wars of Edward II'; Falcandus; Guisborough; Higden; Huntingdon; Jumièges; Lanercost; Malaterra; Malmesbury; Meaux; *Polistorie*; Reading; Simeon; Trokelowe; *Vita Edwardi Secundi*; Worcester, Florence of
Annals of Ireland 52
Annals of London 74, 82, 105
Annals of St Paul's 3, 7, 10, 11, 12, 22, 27, 52, 76, 79, 102, 104, 105, 110, 114
armiger, *see* David; Gaveston
arms:
  captured in Newcastle-upon-Tyne by the earl of Lancaster 87, 90
  surrendered to the king by the earl of Lancaster 91
Arnaud, lord of Gabaston, knight, father of Piers Gaveston:
  hostage for Edward I in Aragon 4
  hostage for Edward I in France 4; escapes to England 4, 10
  his part in Edward I's Welsh campaign (of 1282–3) 4
  wife of, *see* Marsan, Clarmonde de
Arundel:
  Edmund fitz Alan, earl of: at Warwick Castle 88; witness to the charter granting the earldom of Cornwall to Gaveston 31; witness to other royal charters 31 n. 53
  Richard fitz Alan, earl of: carries the crown of St Edward at Richard II's coronation 42 n. 97
Ashwell, Guy de, monk of Westminster:
  letters of Roger de Aldenham to 67–8, 115–18, 123–4
  named by Aldenham as a suitable candidate to succeed Wenlok as abbot 61 n. 77, 117
Askeby, Robert de, chancery clerk 40 n. 92